A MANAGER'S GUIDE TO

MARKETING RESEARCH

Survey of Recent Developments

A Manager's Guide to Marketing Research

Survey of Recent Developments

PAUL E. GREEN

and

RONALD E. FRANK

Wharton School of Finance and Commerce
University of Pennsylvania

JOHN WILEY & SONS, INC.

New York · London · Sydney

To the Memory of

WROE ALDERSON

Who could do, teach—and

teach teachers, as well.

Series Foreword

In an era in which management science and technology are growing rapidly and at the same time causing great change one thing remains constant—the manager's need to stay informed. To fulfill his need and to master the new techniques, the manager must understand their workings, grasp their potentials and limitations, and know what questions to ask to ensure that a most efficient job will be done.

This is the premise on which the Manager's Guide Series is based and on which each book is written. The subjects are presented in such a manner as to provide ease of understanding, a grasp of terminology, and a comprehension of potential applications. This approach should enable the manager to understand better the techniques of the management sciences and to apply them to his own needs not as a practitioner but as a mature administrator.

Preface

THIS SHORT and nontechnical book has been written primarily for the "consumer" of marketing research—the business executive. Our objectives and methods of presentation are set forth in more detail in the Introduction. We hope that this small volume will contribute toward the manager's understanding of what is happening in the development of marketing research technique and its implications for improved decision making. We have tried to take a balanced approach by discussing the limitations as well as the advantages associated with these recent developments.

Our debt to Professor Russell L. Ackoff, of the University of Pennsylvania, is considerable. He not only suggested the basic idea but provided a model for us, namely, *A Manager's Guide to Operations Research* (coauthored with Patrick Rivett and published by John Wiley and Sons, 1964). He was also kind enough to review and comment critically on the completed manuscript.

We acknowledge the helpful comments of Professor Harper W. Boyd, Jr., Stanford University, and Patrick J. Robinson, Marketing Science Institute. Although we have not always been "guided" by the comments of our reviewers, we are grateful for their suggestions.

Material for this book has been gathered from many sources, including our own writings. We have tried to select material—whatever the source—to convey the substance of the concepts in a direct and matter-of-fact manner. Our dependence on the contributions of many marketing researchers—practitioners and academicians alike—will rapidly become apparent to the reader as we discuss various developments in this field.

Finally, we would like to thank Mollie Horowits, who typed the manuscript, and our wives Betty and Iris, who graciously put up with the interruptions to family life that invariably accompany book writing.

Philadelphia, Pennsylvania
January 1967

PAUL E. GREEN
RONALD E. FRANK

Contents

A MANAGER'S GUIDE TO

MARKETING RESEARCH

Survey of Recent Developments

Introduction

As an organized activity, marketing research is scarcely more than 50 years old. Despite its relative "youth," however, there are indications that this function is already undergoing a substantial change in the diversity and sophistication of its techniques. This change in method and tactics has stemmed from two sources:

1. The *need* for better analytical procedures has grown as decision making in marketing has become more risky and critical to corporate survival and growth.
2. The *capacity* for solving more difficult managerial problems has been increased by recent developments in related disciplines, particularly applied mathematics and the behavioral sciences.

This book is concerned with these changes and their implications for the theory and practice of marketing research, current and future. As its title implies, it is *not* a comprehensive text in marketing research but rather a discussion of recent developments in method and technique. Our hoped-for audience is the "nonspecialist" — the line or staff executive, marketing or otherwise — who, although reasonably familiar with traditional marketing research procedures, has not been exposed to more recent advances in the field. We assume that he is interested in obtaining a brief, nontechnical description of the newer techniques in terms of their purpose, assumption structure, range of applicability, and efficiency, compared with more traditional procedures.

Moreover, we have employed the words "guide" and "survey" deliberately. Since this book can give only limited coverage to the field, we felt that part of our responsibility was to provide the reader with more comprehensive references and source material. It is our hope that some of these selected references will be followed up by the reader who desires a more complete description than the scope of our coverage supplies.

A few words should also be said about what this book is not.

First, it is not a compendium of "case studies," successful or otherwise. Although we do discuss some applications from time to time, reported usage of many of these techniques has been low to date. This is due partly to the confidential nature of most of the applications that have been made and partly to the fact that many of the techniques are still in the developmental stage.

Second, this book is not an exhortative plea for the (uncritical) adoption of these procedures. In our judgment such "hard-sell" tactics are both silly and insulting to the experienced executive. These techniques have obvious limitations; we are confident, however, that their advantages are sufficient to justify the time spent in becoming aware of what they can and cannot do.

Finally, "newness" is a relative term. To some managers some of the techniques will not be considered novel. Our inclusion of material is bound, to a large extent, to be arbitrary, but we hope that our discussion will provide something new for most managers. In our zeal to stress "innovations," however, we do not wish to convey the impression that the bread-and-butter procedures of survey design, questionnaire preparation, and the compilation of sales statistics are outmoded. Quite the contrary; *most* of the typical marketing researcher's time will continue to be spent on these activities. But we believe that he will be doing other things as well, particularly in the direction suggested by the developments described in the following chapters.

Format and Style

The book is divided into six chapters. Chapter 1 mainly discusses one major development — the conceptualization of marketing research in terms of the cost versus value of information supplied by this activity. With the advent of modern decision theory, it now appears possible to measure the contribution of marketing research in economic terms. This strategic view of marketing research will eventually lead to marked changes in the administration of this activity and its allocation over alternative projects competing for research effort. Chapter 1 thus represents an overview for the rest of the book and has been prepared primarily for the line manager.

Chapter 2 describes recent developments in attitudinal measurement techniques and other approaches drawn from the behavioral sciences. In this chapter we discuss the increasing role which the behavioral sciences are beginning to play in the quantification of buyer perception, motivation, and choice. We discuss such techniques as psychological scaling, experimental gaming, and related techniques in the measurement of buyer preferences.

In Chapter 3 our attention is directed toward innovations in the use of experimental design procedures and various techniques from applied statistics for analyzing large masses of interrelated data. In this chapter we describe developments in statistically designed experiments and multivariate statistical procedures and their implications for determining the impact of alternative marketing strategies on buyer behavior and sales response.

Chapter 4 presents a discussion of marketing "models" and techniques for describing marketing processes and controlling sales effort expenditures. Techniques such as mathematical programming, Markov processes, and simulation are finding increasing application in the solution of marketing problems involving media scheduling, new product introduction, and the like. Although many of these procedures were originally proposed by operations researchers, the responsibility for further design and implementation of these techniques is being assumed to an increasing extent by marketing research practitioners.

In Chapter 5 we present a prognostication of "things to come" and the implications of our speculations for the staffing, administration, and training of future marketing research groups. As might be guessed already, it is our belief that the marketing researcher of the future will be "at home" in both quantitative and behavioral methods.

Chapter 6 represents our brief "guide" to the literature for the reader who wants to acquire more (and continuing) information about these recent developments.

Finally, a word on style is appropriate. Inasmuch as the book has been prepared primarily for the business executive, we have tried to refrain from the rather formalized presentation typically associated with textbook writing. Footnotes have been cut to a minimum; our indebtedness to the literature has been handled through citation of appropriate references which appear in the bibliography. The book contains very few formulas and no mathematical proofs. End-of-chapter exercises and other textbook devices have been omitted.

We do hope that the reader will find the style lively and concise — without the dogmatic overtones that such brevity frequently invites. Many of the developments taking place in marketing measurement and analysis are no less than exciting. If we can convey some of this excitement — *without* glossing over the limitations of current techniques — we feel that our objective will have been achieved. If we can instruct a bit, as well as motivate, our objective will have been surpassed.

I Marketing Research and the Economics of Information

Introduction

One of the most significant recent developments in marketing research concerns the change that is taking place in the *evaluation* of this activity as an information-supplying function for managerial decision making. With the advent of modern statistical decision theory, it is now possible to measure the value of marketing research within an economics-of-information framework. This approach implies a fundamental change in the planning and control of this activity and provides guidance for answering the critical question: how much to spend for marketing research? As such, this topic is of prime importance to the consumer of marketing research information — the business executive.

In this chapter we first discuss the purposes of research within the context of marketing decision making. We then summarize briefly the evolution of marketing research in terms of the events that have taken place over the last several decades in the practice of business management. These trends have culminated in a de-emphasis on the "fact-gathering" role of research. There is a growing awareness of the value of marketing research as viewed in the context of *marketing intelligence* systems and their relationship to managerial problem formulation and analysis.

We then describe the analytical apparatus — statistical decision theory — which has provided a means for orienting marketing research within a cost-versus-value-of-information framework. We discuss the implications of this new orientation for managerial problem solving and the administration of the marketing research activity. We conclude our discussion with an appraisal of the

5

current stage of implementation of this concept and the future outlook for its application to research planning and control.

The Nature and Development of Marketing Research

The functions of marketing research naturally derive from the *problems* of marketing. Stated succinctly, these problems, subject to profit considerations, can be characterized as follows:

What to sell?
To whom to sell?
When to sell it?
How to sell it?

Attempts to answer these deceptively simple questions have given rise to a host of marketing staff activities, such as product and service planning, customer and channel research, distribution cost research, and media planning.

Whether we use the familiar term, "marketing research," or the newer (and more esoteric) label, "marketing intelligence," the fact remains that the purpose of the activity is to *provide information useful for the identification and solution of marketing problems.* As we shall show, however, marketing research has undergone quite an evolution in terms of its importance to management decision making, its methods of inquiry, and the means by which its contribution can be measured.

Evolution of marketing research

Today, marketing research is big business. Recent estimates indicate that more than $200 million is being spent annually by business in the United States on this activity. Expenditures on marketing research by consumer goods manufacturers have been doubling approximately every five years. Outlays by industrial goods makers are increasing almost 50 per cent per five-year period [28].

Formal marketing research activities can also be found in advertising agencies, wholesale and retail organizations, various service firms (such as insurance companies, banks, real estate agencies), and the mass communications media. In addition, such diverse institutions as libraries, colleges, social agencies, and hospitals have availed themselves of marketing research. National, state, and local governments are frequent users as well. Marketing research has permeated almost every facet of our nation's activity, from religious organizations to pari-mutuel horse-racing establishments.

Why this burgeoning of growth and proliferation of marketing research into virtually every social and business institution of the economy? Undoubtedly the increasing use of marketing research has reflected the growing importance of the marketing function itself in the overall operation of business firms. Since 1911, when Charles C. Parlin founded the first formal marketing research department at the Curtis Publishing Company, the posture of business firms has increasingly assumed a *marketing,* as opposed to production, orientation. Concomitant with this change in functional importance has been the shift in marketing research activity from the tabulation of published data and one-shot consumer surveys to continuous and sophisticated research effort on all phases of marketing from product planning and diversification to advertising copy testing and package design.

Although the private consulting firms in the field — for example, A. C. Nielsen, Audits and Surveys, Alfred Politz, Market Facts, Market Research Corporation of America, and National Analysts — still loom large in the overall research picture, two trends in the *sources* of marketing research activity are apparent. First, more business firms are developing internal competence for performing many marketing research operations, formerly farmed out to outside consultants. Second, the old, established full-line consulting firms are being challenged by the appearance of specialty firms such as Social Research, Inc., and Simulmatics, Inc., whose services have grown up around some innovation in research methodology.

Today's marketing manager is thus faced with an increasing variety of suppliers of marketing research services. In addition to expansion in the types of services available, events are taking place which are heightening the manager's need for operational procedures that appraise the potential value of alternative marketing research services.

As business firms have moved from a production to marketing orientation, there has been an attendant increase in problem complexity and lack of control over the outcomes of decisions. In the functional areas of manufacturing, equipment maintenance, materials handling, and quality control decisions are based largely on cost considerations. The marketing executive, however, must consider both demand and cost factors. The complexity and high uncertainty associated with the outcomes of decisions involving price, advertising, distribution channel selection, and product development are in large part due to our lack of understanding of demand relationships. The manager must cope with an expanded environment which embraces the industry in which the firm competes [89] and, frequently, the national and world economy as well.

With this shift in emphasis from the internal to the external environment of the firm, the marketing manager also faces a comparative shortage of relevant information that is ordinarily available from internal accounting and production records. Not only is it difficult to assemble data on the outcomes of marketing actions, but the information which can be made available tends to be perishable in quality and costly to obtain.

As a consequence of the scarcity and perishability of commercial information, the riskiness of decisions in marketing tends to be higher than those in most of the other functional areas of management. Moreover, in contrast to his production counterpart, the marketing manager has little opportunity to exercise "stop-loss" control if things go awry. An unexpected move by a competitor, a change in consumer tastes, or a balky group of distributors may upset the most carefully planned marketing strategy with little opportunity for "shutting down the line" until the trouble is fixed.

Marketing problems can thus be characterized as complex, predominantly behavioral, relationships between the firm and its environment (with a resultant lack of control over outcomes) where information about environmental conditions is subject to rapid obsolescence and is expensive to assemble. Finally, the absolute size of marketing and distribution expenditures — estimated to amount to over half of the typical firm's expenditures — is demonstration enough that the stakes as well as the uncertainty of marketing decisions are high.

Decision Theory and the Economics of Information

As already indicated, today's marketing manager is being faced with both a growing number of specialized services for performing marketing research and an increased need for obtaining relevant information about the consequences of alternative marketing courses of action (which themselves are increasing in scope and complexity). What would appear to be needed is some framework for measuring the effectiveness of alternative marketing research studies. Fortunately, such a framework has recently become available from the field of applied statistics. Discussion of this model and its relationship to the problem of appraising the productivity of marketing research — or information gathering in general — comprises the remainder of this chapter. We cover, in turn, the essentials of statistical decision theory, its relevance to measuring the net value of marketing research, and finally the implications of this approach for marketing research planning, administration, and control.

The essentials of statistical decision theory

Statistical methodology is no stranger to the marketing researcher. The computation of averages and measures of dispersion as well as the use of probability sampling has been commonplace in marketing research almost since its inception. What is new to marketing research, however, is the increasing emphasis being placed on *analytical* — as opposed to descriptive — statistics. Statistical methodology, itself, is undergoing reformulation and is now being commonly referred to as "the science of making wise decisions in the face of uncertainty" [147]. For the practical business man, the books by Schlaifer [150] and Chernoff and Moses [33], both of which appeared as late as 1959, stand out as key references. Since the appearance of these innovative texts, several articles [18, 30, 78, 148] have shown the connection between this reorientation of statistics and the measurement of marketing research productivity.

Ironically, some of the underpinnings of "Bayesian decision theory" (the name given to this new statistical approach) were laid more than 200 years ago when an English clergyman, Thomas Bayes, proposed a procedure for combining new information about the likelihood of alternative "states of nature" (that is, descriptions of the real world) being the true state of affairs with probabilities existing *before* the receipt of the new information. Although modern Bayesian theory bears little relationship to Thomas Bayes' pioneering work, the name has stuck.

Virtually all decision making — marketing or otherwise — takes place under conditions of (at least partial) ignorance about the variables that will influence the consequences of the decision. Will the new product, now undergoing test marketing fail or succeed if introduced nationally? Will ad *A* or ad *B* pull more reader attention? If we raise the price of our product's economy package by five cents, what will happen to unit sales volume and profits? The illustrations are endless.

Like it or not, the marketing manager is usually forced to *gamble* and consequently runs the risk of making wrong decisions. Of course, the more certain he is of the outcomes, the lower his risk. Moreover, the better some course of action is over competing options, under a wide variety of possible environmental conditions, the less is the risk of incurring sizable costs if he *is* wrong.

Frequently the marketing manager can avail himself of additional information related to the consequences of the alternatives being considered. Usually the information is not perfectly accurate and costs something to collect and analyze. Moreover, the manager frequently has available *several* information-gathering options of varying cost and accuracy. The questions which Bayesian decision theory is designed to answer are basically two:

1. How should the manager choose among alternative information-gathering options, including the option of gathering no additional information at all?
2. Having made this choice, how should a terminal (as opposed to information-buying) act be chosen with or without the additional information?

Behind these preceding common-sense questions there exists a large body of detailed and technical theory. Our purpose here is to discuss only the barest outlines of the Bayesian approach, by means of a simple gambling example. We shall then try to take a broad step from this artificial world to the *real* environment of managerial decision making and marketing research, now viewed as a cost-incurring (and fallible) information supplier.

A Simplified Application of Bayesian Decision Theory

One nice thing about gambling illustrations is that they have almost universal appeal even if the context seems artificial and overly abstract. The following "game," taken from Green [79], nevertheless contains all the essential concepts of Bayesian decision theory; that is, its *structure* is similar to many real-world marketing problems although its content is rather trivial.

Assume that we have three small boxes which we shall call *A*, *B*, and *C*. Outwardly the boxes look alike. We are told that box *A* contains two gold coins, box *B* contains a gold and a silver coin, and box *C* contains two silver coins. The boxes are put in random order on a table top, and we are allowed to perform a simple "experiment," namely, to choose a box at random and, without observing the contents of the box, draw a single coin. Suppose that the coin drawn happens to be gold. Based on this "experimental" evidence we are asked to state the probability that the remaining coin is also gold, that is, that box *A* was chosen.

We can reason as follows. Before we were given the datum that the first coin drawn was gold, our prior probability of drawing box *A* was one-third. This assumes that our state of knowledge with respect to the characteristics of each box led to a special case of this approach, the assignment of an equally likely measure over all states of nature: *A*, *B*, and *C*. (A person who thinks that he possesses extrasensory perception might not wish to make an equiprobable assignment at all; Bayes's theorem handles either case.)

We can next ask ourselves the following question: Given the choice of each box, *A*, *B*, and *C*, respectively, how likely is it that we would have observed a gold coin? Had we chosen box *A* it is clear that we must observe a gold coin on a single draw from the box since *both* coins in *A* are gold; thus a probability of unity is correct. Given that box *B* was chosen, the probability is one-half that our first draw would have produced a gold coin, since box *B* contained one gold and one silver coin. Given that we chose box *C*, it is clear that the chances of drawing a gold coin are zero, since both coins in *C* are silver. These probabilities are called "conditional" probabilities. For example, the probability of drawing a gold coin, conditional upon having picked up box *B*, is one-half.

From here it is but a short step to Bayes' theorem. Figure 1.1 shows a diagrammatic representation of the problem. The area of the rectangle is first divided into three vertical strips of equal area, which represent the prior probabilities of drawing box *A*,

B, or *C.* Next the conditional probabilities are pictured by shading the area of each strip in proportion to the probability of observing a gold coin. Thus all of strip *A* is shaded, half of strip *B* is shaded, and none of strip *C* is shaded.

Since in performing our "experiment" we have *observed* a gold coin, we must *revise* our prior probabilities to reflect this new information; that is, *only* the shaded area is now relevant. Moreover, the shaded area under each vertical strip represents the combined occurrence of (1) choosing a particular box and (2) getting a gold coin. These are joint events. Now, if we divide the *shaded* area between the relevant boxes *A* and *B,* it is clear that two thirds of *this* total area is contained in the vertical strip *A;* hence the re-

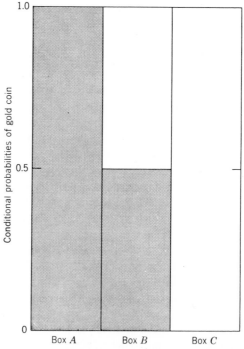

Fig. 1.1   Box problem: pictorial representation of probabilities. Reprinted, with permission, from P. E. Green, "Bayesian Decision Theory in Advertising," *Journal of Advertising Research,* Vol. 2, No. 4 (December 1962), pp. 33–41.

vised probability of having drawn box A is now two thirds versus a one third probability of having drawn box B. Obviously, given our information that the coin is gold, we have *not* drawn box C.

Bayes' theorem merely formalizes this approach. Suppose we wanted to find, for example, the probability that box A was drawn, given the observance of a gold coin. We can use the following formula (Bayes' theorem), where $P(g \mid A)$ stands for the conditional probability of a gold coin, given that we have drawn box A; $P(A)$ stands for the probability of drawing box A in the first place; and $P(A \mid g)$ stands for the conditional probability of having drawn box A, given the information that the coin was gold. Other symbols are defined analogously.

$$P(A \mid g) = \frac{P(g \mid A) \cdot P(A)}{P(g \mid A) \cdot P(A) + P(g \mid B) \cdot P(B) + P(g \mid C) \cdot P(C)}$$

$$= \frac{1 \cdot \frac{1}{3}}{(1 \cdot \frac{1}{3}) + (\frac{1}{2} \cdot \frac{1}{3}) + (0 \cdot \frac{1}{3})}$$

$$= \frac{2}{3}$$

From our previous discussion we already know that this solution, $\frac{2}{3}$, agrees with our intuitive analysis of the problem. Notice that the revised or "posterior" probability is conditional upon a *particular* observed event; the appearance of a silver coin would have changed the posterior probability assigned to box A from two-thirds, under the gold coin case, to zero.

So much for probability revision. We must now determine how the approach is used in evaluating courses of action. The criterion for choosing among courses of action under the Bayesian approach is actually quite simple: choose the act that leads to the highest expected or, in effect, weighted average payoff. We can modify our example to illustrate this criterion.

Assume that we have the option to bet or not bet that we will choose box A from the three boxes on the table. Suppose we would win $1.00 if A were drawn, but would lose $.60 if box B were drawn and would lose $.50 were we to draw box C. Suppose further that we are not allowed to run an "experiment" before betting, that is, not allowed to observe one of the two coins in each box.

A pictorial representation of these initial ground rules appears

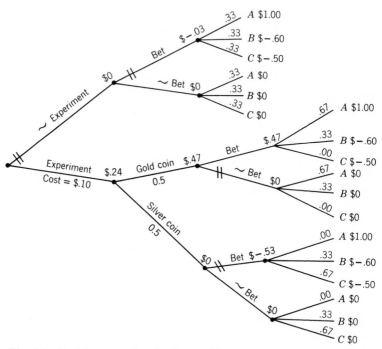

Fig. 1.2 Decision tree: box betting problem. Reprinted, with permission, from P. E. Green, "Bayesian Decision Theory in Advertising," *Journal of Advertising Research,* Vol. 2, No. 4 (December 1962), pp. 33–41.

in the upper branch of the "tree" diagram shown in Fig. 1.2. Looking at the extreme right of the upper branch, we note the conditional payoffs, namely, $1.00, $—.60, and $—.50, associated with drawing box *A, B,* and *C,* respectively. To find the *expected* payoff associated with "bet," we merely multiply these payoffs by our prior probabilities, ⅓, ⅓, and ⅓, and sum the products, leading to a negative expected payoff of $—.03; that is, we would lose, three cents per bet, on the average. Obviously, if maximizing expected monetary value is our criterion we would select the "no bet" action with an expected payoff of zero.

Consider another modification of the problem. Assume that *before* we decide whether to bet or not we are allowed to observe one coin from the box chosen. To conduct this "experiment" we are charged $.10. Conditional payoffs are the same as before. The major difference is that we can delay our choice of whether to bet or not until *after* we have observed the results of our experiment and it will cost us $.10 to run the experiment.

The lower branch of the "tree" diagram of Fig. 1.2 summarizes the features of this strategy. If we look at the extreme right portion of the lower branch, following the sub-branch labeled "gold coin," we note the probabilities: .67, .33, and .00. These represent the posterior probabilities derived from applying Bayes' theorem on the assumption that a gold coin is observed. Notice that the expected payoff associated with "bet" is $.47, clearly higher than that associated with "do not bet." Therefore the double slash through the "no bet" sub-branch indicates that if we observed a gold coin we would choose the "bet" rather than "no bet" act.

Before the fact, however, it is possible that we may observe a silver rather than a gold coin. If we follow this branch and look at the posterior probabilities — .00, .33, and .67 for *A, B,* and *C,* respectively — the expected payoff associated with "betting" is very poor, namely, $—.53. It is clearly to our advantage *not* to bet if we observe a silver coin; hence the double slash through the "bet" sub-branch. But we must still compute the probabilities of getting a gold versus silver coin. These are known as marginal probabilities and their calculation along with the calculation of joint probabilities is shown in Table 1.1.

Now we may obtain the expected payoff of $.24 by again averaging over the payoffs associated with the *best* act taken after the observance of each possible result of the experiment, that is, $.24 = (0.5 × $.47) + (0.5 × $0). The expected payoff must then be reduced by $.10, the cost incurred in using this strategy,

Table **1.1**   Calculation of Joint and Marginal Probabilities for the Box Problem

	Box A		Box B		Box C		Marginal
Gold Coin	$\frac{1}{3}$	+	$\frac{1}{6}$	+	0	=	$\frac{1}{2}$
Silver Coin	0	+	$\frac{1}{6}$	+	$\frac{1}{3}$	=	$\frac{1}{2}$
Marginal	$\frac{1}{3}$	+	$\frac{1}{3}$	+	$\frac{1}{3}$	=	1

leading to a *net* expected payoff of $.14. This figure is still higher than the $0 associated with the best act under "do not experiment"; hence we double slash the upper main branch of the tree.

To summarize, our best strategy is to (a) conduct our experiment and (b) then take the best act after observing the experimental results. If we do this, our average payoff per play, after deducting the cost of the experiment, is $.14.

Before leaving this example, let us introduce one additional complication. Suppose we could enlist the services of a "shill" who, for a payment of $.25, could secretly give us a signal that would indicate *without error* the nature of the box we picked up before we had to decide whether or not to bet. What is the net value of this *perfect* information?

Inasmuch as the shill cannot influence our choice process (but only tell us *after* we have picked up a box which box it is) about one third of the time we will pick up box *A* and, being given its identification, will decide to bet. We will make $1.00. Two thirds of the time we will pick up box *B* or box *C* and, upon being told this, will not bet. On these occasions we will make $0. Thus, our average gross payoff per play will be:

$$\tfrac{1}{3} \times \$1.00 + \tfrac{2}{3} \times \$0 = \$.33$$

Since our shill charges $.25 per play for his service, our expected net payoff is only $.33 — $.25, or $.08. *Here is a case where the net value of even perfect information is less than the net value of less reliable (but cheaper) information.*

From gambling game to the real world

As simple as the preceding illustration appears, it nevertheless demonstrates some significant points about the economics of decision making. Consider the situation of an advertising manager faced with the problem of whether or not to increase the level of product advertising in a particular marketing area. Like the gambler, the advertising manager possesses alternative courses of action — a necessary condition in order to have a problem. We may also assume that he wants to achieve certain objectives; he may wish to earn a maximum return on his advertising investment. It is clear that three components of a problem are (a) a decision maker, (b) alternative courses of action, and (c) a means for translating the possible consequences of each action into some measure of the success with which a certain objective or combination of desired objectives is attained.

As our advertising manager reflects on his problem, however he realizes that whereas under some levels of response to increased advertising effort the additional advertising would pay for itself in terms of the profits from increased sales volume, under other levels of response — certainly a zero level — payoffs will be higher if he does not increase his advertising expenditures. Presumably his deliberations include the possible effects of competitors' options for changing their levels of advertising and the resultant impact on total industry sales and his firm's market share. The trouble is that our decision maker does not know for certain the underlying "facts of life" and must deal with payoffs that are conditional upon which of several *possible* events occurs.

In most situations, however, the decision maker has had experience in facing at least broadly analogous situations and has been exposed to the events preceding his particular problem situation of the moment. For example, he may well feel that some of the possible events are more likely to occur than others. Bayesian decision theory merely *formalizes* this notion by assuming that it is possible to assign numerical weights, in the nature of betting odds, such that they obey certain requirements for consistency. In Bayesian parlance, these numerical weights are called *prior probabilities*. Sometimes they may be based on long-run, "objective" experience with very similar problems, whereas in other instances they may be more "subjective." A natural measure for the degree of uncertainty possessed by the decision maker thus becomes the *breadth* of possible states of nature which he feels should be included and the nature of his *probability assignment* over this set of possible events.

But, like our mythical gambler, in many instances the manager can attempt to improve his view regarding the likelihood that each state of nature is the "true" underlying event *before* having to take final action. That is, he may elect to "experiment" before making a terminal choice among alternatives. The advertising manager may conduct a test campaign before deciding whether to increase the total level of promotion.

Gathering additional data usually involves a cost, however, and rarely are data so reliable as to foretell perfectly the true state of nature. Decision makers usually must cope with both experimental (sampling) and systematic error. Thus the manager is forced to weigh the cost of the test campaign against its potential value in supplying information.

As illustrated in the gambling problem, Bayesian decision theory deals with the data collection problem in three principal ways: (a) should additional data be collected at all before choosing a terminal action; (b) given the wisdom of assembling more data, how much data should be collected and in what way; and (c) how can the decision maker revise his prior judgments in the light of this new experimental evidence?

In essence, Bayesian statistics considers the utility or economic consequences attached to alternative acts under different events, the prior judgments of the decision maker regarding the likelihood of occurrence of alternative events, and the potential or actual modification of his prior judgments based on new data. As noted in the gambling illustration, obtaining perfect information — even if possible — may not justify its cost.

For the first time, the activity of marketing research can now be, at least conceptually evaluated in terms of an economics-of-information framework. We believe that this model will exert a significant impact on the design and conduct of marketing research investigations and, indeed, on the organization and administration of the activity itself.

This is not to say, however, that *implementation* of the concepts of Bayesian decision theory is a simple matter. In the simple "box" example, the courses of action, outcomes, payoffs, costs, and reliability of information were given. In actual business applications these components must be identified and structured. We shall have more to say on the critical problems of developing the *inputs* to the Bayesian model in subsequent sections of this chapter.

Implications of decision theory for marketing research evaluation

Several implications stem from the preceding model in which marketing research is viewed as a cost-incurring, information-providing activity. First, the framework emphasizes the key role of *managerial judgment* in the whole problem-solving process and the relationship of marketing research to managerial action. Indeed, the manager is placed in the position of "make or buy" with regard to information; that is, the manager can elect to "make" — use his prior experience and other less formal means of information — or can "buy" additional information through the utilization of marketing research (which frequently can be supplied by internal groups or outside consulting firms).

Second, this kind of orientation also implies that the marketing researcher must work closely with the user of the information to be able to bring his own particular type of expertise to bear on the problem. The marketing researcher's skills can be utilized in a variety of ways within the decision theoretic format. These functions include: (a) problem identification; (b) the search and identification of relevant courses of action; (c) the estimation of alternative consequences of a given course of action and the probabilities associated therewith; and (d) the estimation of the reliabilities and costs of alternative investigations. We examine this *interaction of manager and researcher* for each of these categories, in turn.

Problem Identification. Part of the marketing researcher's responsibility is related to the control of currently pursued courses of action and the identification of problems arising from the failure of present courses of action to achieve desired standards of performance.

An illustration should make this point clear. Suppose an ethical drug firm, an established leader in the production of tranquilizers, is faced with the entry of a new brand by a rival firm. Uncertainty surrounds the new entrant's fate and its repercussions on the established brand. Will it capture a significant share of the market? If so, will this share be taken largely from the market leader's brand? And, again, if so, what can the established leader do about it?

The mere appearance of the new brand on the market might touch off a panic situation in the established firm; or the industry leader may summarily dismiss the new entrant as not having any significant impact on the market. Barring either of these extreme reactions, the established leader, through proper employment of marketing research as a monitoring device, could assemble data on physician-trying rates, re-prescription rates, and attitudes toward the new brand and the competing brands from which the new entrant is garnering business.

The point to be made here is that *two* types of error can be made in establishing the existence of the problem. In the context of this illustration the established firm could assume that the new brand is going to be successful (and in a "panic" mood, overreact) when, in fact, the new entrant will turn out to be a failure. Or, conversely, the established firm could assume that nothing is wrong (the new brand is predicted to fail) when, in fact, the new entrant's success will adversely affect the leader's performance objectives. Systematic monitoring of the new entrant's progress could reduce both risks at a cost which might well be justified by the stakes involved in making a wrong decision based on insufficient data.

The implications of the foregoing situation on the allocation of expenditures for marketing research are not trivial. Time and effort deployed in monitoring the consequences of currently pursued courses of action and the environment of these actions must obviously compete with other marketing research functions.

Search and Identification of Courses of Action. Many so-called "exploratory" studies in marketing research have as their motivation the search for and identification of alternative courses of action. Uncertainty exists in this phase of research activity as well. For example, the search process may be terminated too soon with the consequence that a course of action is selected which is inferior to one that could have been designed had search activity not been terminated too quickly. Conversely, search activity may be carried well beyond the point of diminishing returns.

Returning to our earlier illustration, the established drug firm may conclude (we shall assume correctly) that the new competitive brand will adversely affect its own brand share and profits if the firm does not retaliate in some way. A hasty search for alternatives reveals that a price reduction on the established brand appears desirable. The price change is put into effect. Other firms—including the new entrant firm—counter the price decrease and the trend in brand share is unaffected. Moreover, the total market for the product class is not affected, and the established firm (as well as the other firms) is worse off in profits than it was before.

Suppose, however, that by monitoring the progress of the new entrant, the established firm's marketing research group found that physicians exhibited a high propensity to try the new brand, but that their *repeat* prescription rates were significantly lower, due to the (unexpected) incidence of adverse side effects associated with the new brand. Armed with this information, the established firm could modify its current promotion to stress the "safety" features of its own brand. The objective of this course of action would be to maintain present physician "loyalty," allowing the new entrant to draw proportionately more from competing brands which had not modified their promotional themes.

Here, again, the marketing researcher faces an allocation problem in devoting "proper" effort to the search for courses of action. The point to be made, however, is that the economics of this type of activity can also be evaluated in the light of the Bayesian model and the administrative decision process [23].

Evaluation of the Consequences of Alternative Courses of Action. In the betting problem described earlier, it was assumed that the possible outcomes were known, given that certain events (for example, box was an "*A*" type) occurred. In actual marketing problems a significant portion of the marketing researcher's task may involve his assisting the manager in the estimation of the consequences associated with the occurrence of alternative events as well as the likelihood that certain events will take place. In terms of the ethical drug illustration, the wisdom of changing the advertising theme of the established brand rested on the possible attitudes of physicians toward the relative importance of drug "potency" versus "safety." Marketing research could help to establish the possible ways in which the established firm could retaliate, the possible consequences of each option, and the likelihood of success. Furthermore, this type of *general* information could be used for not only the present decision but perhaps future decisions as well.

Thus, each function of marketing research can, and frequently, does mesh into other functions as problems become identified, structured, and solved. This *process* of problem solving militates against naive application of the decision theoretic model, but does not invalidate its conceptual value.

Estimation of Information Reliability and Cost. The marketing researcher's role in this phase of information valuation is crucial. The marketing manager, with or without the researcher's assistance, may have already identified the problem and formulated alternative courses of action, possible states of nature and their likelihoods, and estimated pertinent consequences. A decision to *delay* immediate action, pending the gathering of additional information, however, presupposes some estimate of the reliability and cost of additional information as well as the costs associated with delay.

The marketing researcher is probably in the best position to give the manager counsel on the reliability of alternative information-gathering activities and their probable costs. He may also be able to supply appropriate advice on the economics of using an internal group versus farming out the study to an outside consulting group. The particular expertise of the marketing researcher is virtually always needed in this phase of the decision process even though the manager's knowledge and experience may be sufficient, on many occasions, to structure the rest of the problem.

The manager-researcher dialogue

The preceding comments imply that the data inputs required in the application of the Bayesian approach are usually best assembled through the *interaction of manager and researcher*. Each can contribute his specific type of knowledge and experience to the formulation and solution of the problem. Although this may sound commonplace, the truth of the matter is that all too frequently the marketing researcher is not asked — even permitted — to assist in the structuring of a managerial problem. Rather, he may be given the type of directive: "Find out all you can about the market for tranquilizers." If the researcher can implement this type of request, he must serve principally as a "fact finder," unaware of the use to which the findings are to be put, the scale of effort to be devoted to the inquiry, and the reliability required in his findings.

Like many models, the value of the Bayesian framework would seem to lie more in the *kinds of questions that its utilization generates* than the kinds of answers it provides. Although applying the model to actual business problems may often require fairly sophisticated procedures — for example, computer simulation, mathematical statistics — the basic logic agrees with common sense. Its major impact is to force the manager and researcher to look at marketing research in terms of its value in reducing the costs of wrong decisions. Dogmatic statements such as: "Take a 10 per cent sample of all households"; "Get the most reliable data available"; and so on, thus become suspect within a framework which attempts to match the value of the information against the cost of acquiring it.

The implications of the Bayesian approach suggest that marketing research studies should be geared to the costs incurred in making decisions in the absence of additional information; that is, the breadth and cost of marketing research studies should relate to *other* components of the decision situation. For example, if prior uncertainty and the costs of wrong decisions are both low, small-scale investigation (or no investigation at all) may be indicated. If the potential information is so unreliable as to be inadequate for reducing prior uncertainty, again the study may not justify its cost. In other instances, of course, the stakes and uncertainty involved in the decision may justify large expenditures for additional information.

Current State of the Bayesian Approach

Now that we have discussed the conceptual basis of the Bayesian model, illustrated its application, and discussed its implications from the standpoint of marketing manager and researcher interaction, some comments should be given on the present stage of its application in industry.

As with any new approach, the time lag between methodological innovation and routine use is frequently long. Reported applications of the approach are still sparse. Green has reported actual applications of the model to problems arising in pricing [81], new product introduction [7], and marketing research [80]. Magee has discussed applications, using the decision tree concept, in capital budgeting [129]. Hertz has discussed applications using a related procedure — dubbed "risk analysis" [103]. We comment briefly on the nature of some of these applications.

New product introduction

In the new product introduction study, management of a large chemical firm was faced with the question of whether to introduce a new product (a packaging material designed for further processing by industrial fabricators) on the basis of the data then available about its chances of commercial success. There were two questions:

1. Should the decision be made "now" versus one year later regarding whether the product should be introduced?
2. Given the answer regarding proper timing of the decision, what size plant and pricing policy should be followed?

The product in question was designed to compete in some 20 end-use markets. Estimates of sales were prepared for three sets of environmental conditions — most probable, optimistic and pessimistic. Three pricing strategies and two plant sizes were considered — in all combinations — as tactical alternatives.

The venture was "run on paper" (in an electronic computer) under a variety of environmental conditions. It turned out that the choice of plant size and pricing policy was insensitive to variations in the environment; that is, given commercialization (now or one year hence) a particular pricing strategy–plant size combination was best. Under the pessimistic set of conditions, however, even this "best" alternative would not yield a satisfactory return.

The second part of the analysis was concerned with the wisdom of delaying commercialization of the new product until one year hence when, presumably, more reliable data could be obtained regarding the chances of the new product's commercial success. Delaying the decision would defer the start of revenues — if the product were successful — and hence the opportunity to earn a return on these cash flows. Moreover, an additional out-of-pocket expense (of $2.6 million) would be involved in keeping the development going and obtaining further commercial data on acceptance of the product by fabricators who were cooperating in end-use tests.

What was not known was the *reliability* that had to be associated with the new data to justify delay of the venture, but the analyst did have enough information to solve for this reliability. The answer turned out to be 90 per cent; that is, management would need almost perfect information regarding the occurrence of the appropriate state of nature to justify delay.

Figure 1.3 shows the structure of the analysis. As can be seen from the tree diagram, given "no delay," the best present decision

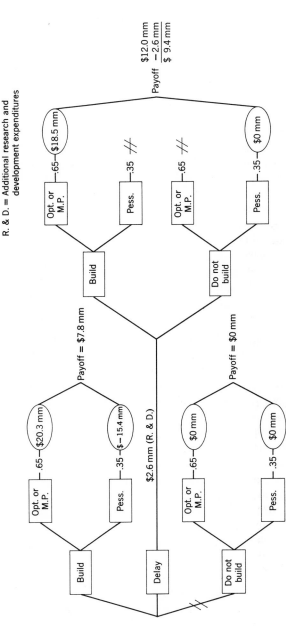

Fig. 1.3 Influence of delay (under perfect future information) on decision to build versus production of product X. Reprinted, with permission, from W. Alderson and P. E. Green, *Planning and Problem Solving in Marketing* (Homewood, Ill.: Richard D. Irwin, 1964), Chapter 8, p. 229.

was to build the (already determined best-size) plant. If so, an expected cash flow of $7.8 million was indicated. Given a one-year delay, *with perfect information,* the payoff could only be increased to $9.4 million. Although the arithmetic is not shown here, this is tantamount to requiring 90 per cent reliable information before a one-year delay option could be justified. The significant point about this application is that management could now appraise the chances of obtaining this required reliability. It was hardly surprising that management in this instance did not feel that information of such high reliability could be secured over the next year. Thus the expected costs of delay exceeded the value of delay.

Capital planning

Magee discusses an application of decision "trees" and Bayesian analysis to a variety of problems in capital planning in which the principal unknowns consist of marketing variables. In one illustration he discusses a problem involving: (a) building a small plant with the later option of expanding the plant, depending on how high a demand for the product materializes; (b) building a large plant (with lower costs per unit of output than could be obtained by two-stage construction); or (c) launching a data-gathering effort and, conditional upon its outcome, taking one of the two possible terminal strategies just enumerated.

Figure 1.4 shows the appropriate tree diagram for the problem faced by the "Stygian Chemical Company" — the name used by Magee in his example. It turned out that in Magee's illustration alternative (c) provided the highest expected present value.

Risk analysis

Hertz's article deals with a topic related to Bayesian analysis— so-called "risk analysis" — which can also be applied to market and financial planning problems. The author first suggests that most of the variables in capital budgeting forecasts (for example, market size, selling prices, market share, required investment) are not known with certainty, particularly the marketing variables. Hertz discusses the development of subjective probability distributions for each key variable to be obtained from experienced executives in the firm. The next step involves simulating the impact of

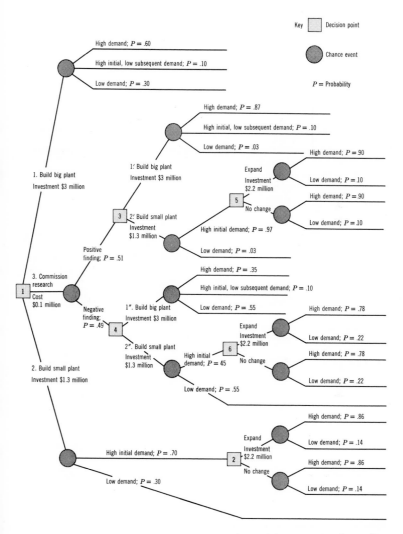

Fig. 1.4 Decision tree for Stygian Chemical with research alternative. Reprinted, with permission, from J. F. Magee, "How to Use Decision Trees in Capital Investment," *Harvard Business Review,* **42** (September-October 1964), pp. 79–96.

27

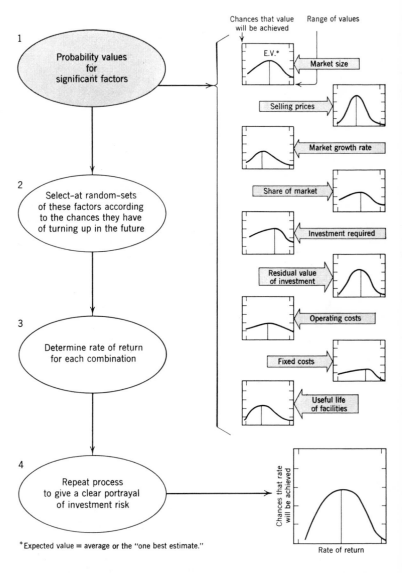

Fig. 1.5 Simulation for investment planning. Reprinted, with permission, from D. B. Hertz, "Risk Analysis in Capital Investment," *Harvard Business Review,* **42** (January-February 1964), pp. 95–106.

possible variations in each of the variables on overall return of the venture. The simulation is performed by a computer.

Figure 1.5 shows a schematic of the method that Hertz describes. Using a Monte Carlo technique (to be described in Chapter 4), Hertz is able to handle a variety of possible probability distributions. The output of the program is a *distribution* of possible returns — each with an associated probability. If management is willing to select an option according to the arithmetic mean of this distribution (or if the distribution is first transformed to index values [178] which reflect management's attitude toward risk) the procedure is similar to Bayesian prior analysis, as already described.

Although the foregoing cases are illustrative of the *potential* for Bayesian decision making in the evaluation of marketing research and/or in general managerial decision making under uncertainty, they do not, of course, indicate the current state of application of the approach by marketing research departments or other industry staff groups.

Extent of use of the Bayesian approach

Unfortunately, no data are available on the extent to which Bayesian analysis is being used. *Published* applications are still few but, owing to the confidential nature of most corporate studies, this is not unusual. We suspect that many, at least many of the large, companies are "experimenting" with the application of the Bayesian approach, but we personally know of only a few firms that have conducted a series of Bayesian-type analyses on planning problems. In virtually all applications of the size and complexity described by the Green, Magee, and Hertz references, recourse to computer simulation was almost a "must" to make the analysis reasonably tractable.

Computer assistance is not as expensive or time consuming (in terms of programming requirements) as it might first appear, however. With the availability of simplified programming techniques, programs that used to take months to prepare can now be done in a matter of days, or even hours. Furthermore, in many types of problems (for example, new venture analysis) a *general* program can be prepared which is easily modifiable to suit individual problems.

The conceptual advantages of the approach

Probably more important than the full-blown application of Bayesian statistics to market planning, marketing research, or whatever, is the growing acceptance of the *concepts* underlying the approach. The authors know of two companies — a large ethical drug firm and a large producer of household products — whose marketing research departments have adopted administrative practices based on Bayesian analysis. The systems of both firms are similar. For example, the drug firm's marketing research department receives many requests by various company personnel in marketing and product development. Before the initiation of a screening process (based on the conceptual foundations of Bayesian decision theory), the department tended to spend too much time on "low-payoff" projects. Marketing research personnel thought that lack of a framework for appraising the potential payoff of research was reducing its overall efficiency.

Accordingly, a procedure was set up in which each person requesting research meets with a senior member of the marketing research department for the purpose of appraising the expected payoff and cost of the proposed research. This dialogue between "client" and "practitioner" has, as its objective, the establishment of: (a) the alternative courses of action under appraisal; (b) the anticipated courses of action which would be taken under various possible outcomes of the research; (c) the prior knowledge that alternative states of nature are true; and (d) the estimated costs of wrong decisions, given that no research is undertaken. It is then up to the researcher to attempt to estimate the reliability and costs of alternative investigations. Although only crude estimates are made of the various inputs to the Bayesian model, the user of the system nevertheless is able to approximate the research costs involved in each study request. Moreover, (seemingly diverse) proposed studies are crosschecked to see if a general study can be devised to answer related questions.

At this writing the system has been in use only a short time. Its principal impact has been to eliminate many low-payoff projects where terminal choices appear to be insensitive to the possible outcomes of the research (as revealed during the "dialogue" process). This experience illustrates one of the primary advantages of explicit models: *a major value of the model lies in forcing the manager to be more rigorous in his own thinking processes,* whether or not unsupported judgments have to enter into the analysis. A formal technique such as this can help the manager to clarify and interrelate the risks he must assume and see where additional information can be most useful for reducing the costs of uncertainty. Perhaps ultimately, more — not less — marketing research may be indicated in many instances. Whatever the result, the significant point is that the procedure can help to quantify a hitherto intangible — *what is the value of information?*

Summary

In this chapter we have tried to examine the marketing research function from a systems point of view — as a cost-incurring service whose purpose is to provide information of potential value for making marketing decisions in the face of uncertainty. With the development of modern decision theory, a model — albeit a recent and still to be fully tested one — is available for measuring the value of marketing research and, hence, how it should be allocated over competing projects. Moreover, *the manager plays a central role* in this process in conjunction with the special expertise of the marketing researcher.

After discussing the rudiments of the Bayesian approach, we commented on some of the problems associated with implementation of the technique and attempted to appraise the current state of its application. In our judgment the Bayesian framework will be most useful in providing a *conceptual* basis for relating the potential value of marketing research to the problem-solving process. We think that this model will play a central role in the design and implementation of marketing research activities of the future. For this reason it seemed fitting to us to introduce the reader to its rationale and implications at the outset of this book.

2 Recent Developments in Behavioral Measurement Techniques

Introduction

Marketing research is making increasing use of concepts and techniques drawn from such behavioral sciences as psychology, sociology, and social-psychology. Terms such as "semantic differential," "Q-sort," and "content analysis" are beginning to find their way into the practice and reporting of marketing research studies as increasingly sophisticated procedures are being employed for predicting behavior. Moreover, marketing research is starting to use some of the *experimental* techniques of the psychologist — for example, the experimental game — in attempting to develop insights about consumer perception, learning, and choice. Goto note

The purpose of this chapter is to discuss some of the attitudinal scaling procedures that have been developed and to report the results of some basic investigations into the buyer choice mechanism. (Although the techniques could be applied to types of behavior other than "buying" behavior, this class of problems is not only illustrative as a context, but represents the focus of attention of most current behavioral research in marketing.) Measuring psychological and sociological phenomena is extremely difficult, and some of the techniques discussed here are still at an early stage of development. Nevertheless, it appears that marketing research will make increasing use of many of these techniques.

We first discuss briefly the policy problems — for example, product and package design and advertising theme and media selection — which underlie the quest for relevant measurements and

32

explanatory models of buyer choice. We then summarize the historical use of those techniques, loosely grouped under the label — "motivation research" — and appraise the current position of clinically based psychological studies in today's marketing research activity.

In the next section of this chapter we comment on the *formal* characteristics of measurement and scales and the various ways in which scaling techniques are classified. We then discuss specific scaling devices (for example, Thurstone's law of comparative judgment, Guttman's scalogram analysis, Stephenson's Q-sort, Osgood's semantic differential) from the standpoint of their underlying assumptions, and their functions in marketing research. We conclude with a discussion of the problems encountered in establishing the reliability and validity of scaling procedures.

We next discuss the rationale and progress to date of various behavioral "models" and miscellaneous techniques that have been proposed for the study of buyer behavior. Illustrations of some experimental games which have been devised for testing some of the behavioral assumptions of these models are also shown.

Finally, we attempt to appraise the current state of application of scaling techniques and behavioral models. Throughout this particular chapter the reader will note a rather cautious attitude on the part of the authors. This may be succinctly stated at the outset: despite the proliferation in marketing research of approaches drawn from the behavioral sciences we still know relatively little about buyer behavior. As will be seen in this chapter, it is much easier to develop attitudinal scales and behavioral models than to establish their reliability and validity over significant ranges of application that are useful for *policy* decisions.

Buying Behavior and Marketing Policy

"Know thy customer" is an old, but nonetheless important, adage of the marketer. We could say, however, that "understand thy customer" is an even more important objective. Of course some set of assumptions about buyer behavior underlies *all* marketing policies, whether the product involved is a low-cost household item or a highly engineered steam turbine. The marketing of such services as insurance, banking, and data processing procedures, is likewise based on some conceptualization of buyers' value systems, needs, and wants.

The study of consumers' attitudes and preferences usually takes up a sizable proportion of total marketing research activity. This type of study has important implications for managerial policy with regard to product design, advertising theme, media selection, and pricing. For example, a brand's "image" may be deficient with regard to some characteristic that can be modified, either physically (in terms of product redesign) or psychologically (in terms of changes in advertising theme).

The quest for consumer attitudinal data is basically related to the questions of *why* people choose certain brands, certain types of media, and certain types of stores, and *why* certain types of advertising messages lead to purchase behavior. For example, one major producer of a packaged food product found through a sociopsychological study of his market that a decided "gap" existed in the spectrum of brands; potential consumers who desired a brand in this category were switching to another closely related product class. Moreover, the firm's advertising messages were stressing a theme that was inconsistent with the psychological characteristics of potential buyers.

The firm acted on both findings by designing a brand that filled in the gap and also by reorienting its advertising theme. Favorable sales results accompanied both changes.

The prediction of buyer behavior from attitudinal data is also important in the development of product line and merchandising strategies which cater to disparate market segments. Quite a bit of empirical research is currently going on in the attempt to determine the personality, socioeconomic, demographic, and lifestyle characteristics associated with brand preferences and their relationship to, and the development of, brand loyalty.

Obviously, if one can develop attitudinal measures that are predictive of brand choice behavior, the implications of such techniques are quite valuable. As we shall show, however, the establishment of these measures has historically been fraught with difficulty.

The evolution of behavioral studies in marketing

The first "invasion" of behaviorists into the domain of marketing research has often been associated with the term "motivation research." (It should be mentioned, however, that the work of the behaviorist, J. B. Watson [179], in the twenties, preceded the influx of the motivation researchers. Watson's application of some of his psychological findings to business led to the employment of repetitive advertising — the incessant, if effective, repetition of slogans, and jingles — in a manner not unlike the classical conditioning experiments of the Russian psychologist, Pavlov.)

Motivation research as evinced in the studies of Dichter [54], Vicary [176], and others, is about a generation old. After a glamorous period in the late forties and early fifties, its current contribution to the business scene has been less auspicious, although several consulting firms are still active in this type of research.

Motivation research can be characterized as the employment of various techniques from clinical psychology — the depth interview, projective tests, focused group interviews — as a means of exploring *why* people exhibit certain kinds of behavior. Motivation researchers attempt to probe the unconscious mind of the buyer. Such research does not always lead to unambiguous conclusions, however. For example, in a celebrated case reported in the *New York Post* (June 1, 1955), Dichter reported some of the reasons why people dislike prunes. Typical of these reasons was the image created by prunes: a "dried-out, worn-out symbol of old age." A competing researcher, Vicary, reported that the fruit has "laxative connotations." Dichter recommended that prunes be renamed "black diamonds" to surround the product with greater prestige. Vicary suggested that the product be advertised for its laxative-inducing effect [Scriven, 152]. (Perhaps both "hunches" were correct for certain subsets of the population.)

The techniques used by motivation researchers rely heavily on "projective" tests; word association, sentence completion, the Rorschach (inkblot test), thematic apperception, cartoons, and the like. As an example of such indirect methods, Steele [163] has reported a study concerned with consumer attitudes regarding milk as a fattening food. Illustrative questions were the following:

1. "A teenager I know likes milk but drinks cokes most of the time. Why do you think she does that?"
2. "If you wanted to encourage her to drink more milk, what would you say to her?"

Mrs. A   Mrs. B

Fig. 2.1 Projective line drawing used in Louisville, Kentucky, Consumer Foods Study, and in Southern Regional Marketing Research Project SM–13. The verbal stimulus accompanying the drawing was as follows: "Would you think that Mrs. A or Mrs. B drank more milk or possibly both about the same amount? (Reason given?)" Reproduced, with permission, from H. L. Steele, "On the Validity of Projective Questions," *Journal of Marketing Research*, **1** (August 1964), pp. 46–49.

In addition, Steele employed a projective line drawing, reproduced in Fig. 2.1. He compared the responses to indirect procedures, as illustrated, with more direct questioning techniques. His findings indicated that indirect questioning procedures produced responses different from those obtained by direct methods. Furthermore, attitudes as elicited from the indirect procedures appeared to be *more valid* predictors of milk consumption. Apparently the more direct questioning procedure tended to raise various inhibitions about obesity and milk consumption, with a resultant distortion of responses.

The current place of motivation research in marketing

As might be expected, many criticisms have been leveled against the procedures used by motivation researchers. Most of the adverse comments have stemmed from practitioners employing more traditional sampling techniques and structured questionnaires. Illustrations of these criticisms are the following:

1. Techniques borrowed from clinical psychologists whose concern is with abnormalities of human behavior are not relevant for the study of "normal" behavior.
2. Even trained psychologists require that depth interview techniques be extended over a lengthy period before valid insights into the unconscious can be obtained. One- or two-hour "depth" interviews cannot accomplish this result.
3. Depth interviewing and other motivational research techniques are time consuming and expensive, leading to the necessity for small, nonprobability samples. The results are difficult, if possible at all, to project to the whole population of interest.
4. Methods emphasizing the single-case approach do not give sufficient information on *dominant* buying motives. Such information is needed to design advertising campaigns and products to appeal to large segments of the market.

The controversy between clinician and statistician has subsided somewhat during the last few years. Motivation research no longer holds the limelight it once did. Nevertheless, the projective techniques of motivation researchers are gaining use and acceptance, but largely as procedures for *exploratory* research and the development of hypotheses for testing via more structured, probability sampling plans. After its initial flurry of attention, motivation research has been assimilated into the market researcher's *modus operandi*, and the once-bitter controversy over its pros and cons has largely abated.

The quest for new measurement techniques continues, however. Some of the techniques of "psychophysics" (the measurement of psychological responses to various stimuli) are finding their way into marketing research investigations. We shall discuss some of these innovations after first describing some of the formal properties of measurement and scales.

Some Formal Properties of Scales

Marketing researchers are becoming more self-conscious about the assumptions underlying their measurement techniques. Unlike the carpenter who works with such well-defined measures as length, weight, and volume, the marketing researcher must frequently deal with attitudinal data. Whereas the carpenter can "add" two one-foot boards to span a two-foot space, it frequently is not clear what responses to certain attitudinal statements of the type: "Brand A is preferable to brand B with respect to attribute X" really mean. For example, can we state how much better; can the statement be applied to all consumers; and can we predict what will happen if brand B is "improved" with respect to attribute X?

Measurement

Measurement is a field of interest to all the sciences, but it is only during the past decade or so that marketing researchers have paid serious attention to the properties of scales that have been developed in the course of attempting to measure various aspects of human behavior. As we shall show, much of this impetus has stemmed from the work undertaken by experimental psychologists, but even so the marketing researcher (and behavioral scientist as well) must frequently settle for less informative scales than are typically found in the physical sciences.

As expressed by Ackoff [1], measurement "is a way of obtaining symbols to represent the properties of objects, events or states, which symbols have the same relevant relationship to each other as do the things which are represented." In measurement, then, we are interested in the correspondence between certain empirical entities and a formal model (usually a number system) in terms of the relationships that are presumed to exist among the elements of each system. In the behavioral field, however, the analyst must frequently deal with *indicants* of these properties. For example, we may talk about the property, "achievement," in terms of a specified number of correct answers on some written test. Similarly, "intelligence" or "ascendency" may be defined in terms of answers to certain test batteries. If so, the indicant represents the test score; the term "construct" is frequently used to describe the property that the indicant purports to measure.

Types of scales

What we usually refer to as a "scale" is technically a ratio scale (weight, height) which contains a natural zero and constant unit of measurement. It is easy for us to go from one unit, say yards, to another unit, say feet, by a simple conversion ratio. Moreover, the concept of "zero" yards (or feet) is a natural origin on both scales. In the behavioral field, such scales are much more rare. It is usually not meaningful to state that "Jones is twice as intelligent as Smith" or that "this brand of canned peas is twice as tasty as that brand."

Scales are usually classified into the following principal categories: (a) nominal, (b) ordinal, (c) interval, and (d) ratio. Each scale possesses a set of underlying assumptions and admissible operations. This categorization also represents progression from "weak" properties (nominal scales) to "strong" properties (ratio scales).

Nominal scales provide the barest of information, for numbers serve only as labels to identify the properties under study. Nominal scales are used in a variety of ways — classifying books in a library, identifying baseball players, telephone subscribers, credit card customers, and the like. All the members of the class are assigned the same number and no two classes are given the same number. All we have to do to use nominal scaling is to be able to tell when entities are "equal" or "not equal" with respect to specific properties. It is meaningless to add the numbers or even to order them since we are merely using the numerals as "shorthand" for more verbalized (but more lengthy) descriptions.

Ordinal scales require that the objects can be rank ordered according to some attribute or property. If we rank five brands of beer according to "quenchability," the resultant numbers (say, 1, 2, 3, 4, 5) indicate *only* rank order. A different sequence (say, 2, 4, 8, 10, 20) would serve just as well since an ordinal scale does not assume equal intervals between the numbers or, indeed, even that some object has "none" of the property being measured. It is meaningless to add ranks or to say, for example, that the difference between the pair ranked 2 and 4 is equal to the difference between the pair ranked 8 and 10. Ordinal scales do possess all the properties of nominal scales since two entities with the same "amount" of the characteristic would presumably receive the same rank.

Interval scales imply that numerically equal distances on the scale represent equal distances (a constant measurement unit) in the property being measured. In this type of scale it is meaningful to talk about adding and subtracting *intervals* as well as taking ratios of *differences* between scale values. For example, if we had the scale values 1, 2, 3, 4, 5 for five brands of beer, measured according to "foaminess," it is meaningful to say that the difference between the brand scored 1 and the brand scored 3 is equal to the difference between the brand scored 3 and the brand scored 5. We *cannot* state, however, that the brand scored 2 is twice as foamy as the brand scored 1; this would require a natural zero.

The measurement of temperature represents a common application of interval scaling. We remember, of course, that converting Fahrenheit to centigrade involves the formula

$$T_c = \frac{5}{9} \, (T_f - 32)$$

in which an arbitrary constant (32) appears in the formula. We call this a linear equation and state that interval scales are unique only up to a linear transformation.

Ratio scales permit us to perform all the usual arithmetic operations on scale values since we assume that a natural origin or zero exists as well as a constant unit of measurement. Scale numbers exhibit the actual amount of the property (gallons, inches, etc.) being measured. For example, we could measure the weight of salt contained in a standard container of a specified brand of beer and state whether this brand had "twice as much" saltiness — in this physical, not psychological, sense — as some other similarly measured brand. Ratio scales thus contain all the properties of "lower" forms of scaling and more besides.

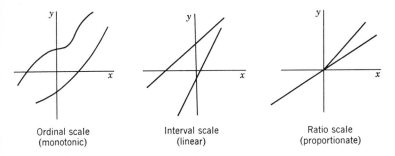

Fig. 2.2   Permissible transformations of various scales.

Some idea of the permissible transformations which can be performed on ordinal, interval, and ratio scales can be noted from Fig. 2.2. If we let x stand for the original scale value, we note that the values of y also fulfill the scale's requirements. An ordinal scale can be transformed into any set of numbers that is monotonically (order preserving) increasing. Transformation of an interval scale is restricted to a positive linear transformation and transformation of a ratio scale is confined to a positive proportionate transformation (through the intersection of the axes).

Before leaving the subject of the formal properties of various types of scales, we should point out that most of the ordinary statistical operations (computation of arithmetic means, standard deviations) and significance tests (t test, F test) require that the data be at least interval scaled. Stevens [166] points out some of the dangers of conducting the usual statistical tests on data that do not meet these requirements.

A Classification of Scaling Methods

Much of what is now known about scaling techniques has evolved from the early work of psychometricians. Most of this pioneering work (some conducted as early as the mid-1800's) involved the study of psychological relationships to physical stimuli, for example, pitch, loudness, and brightness, and is associated with the names of Weber and Fechner. In this century, largely starting with the work of Thurstone [170], methods have been developed for measuring psychological responses to nonphysical stimuli such as attitudinal questions, corporate names, trademarks, advertising copy, and package designs.

In this section we describe briefly the principal methods used to derive scales and comment on their underlying assumptions and limitations. Although there are many ways of classifying scales, we shall concentrate on the basic dichotomy proposed by Torgerson [172]:

1. Judgment methods — assume that the attribute is designated in advance, and that the subject judges the stimuli only with regard to the intensity of the attribute; whether or not the subject "agrees" with the attributes is assumed to be irrelevant. The subject attempts to order the stimuli along some continuum of this attribute. In these methods only the stimuli — not the subjects — are scaled.
2. Response methods — assume that the attribute is not prespecified for the subject. Both stimuli and subjects are scaled with regard to some assumed attribute which is not stated in the instructions.

As might be inferred from the foregoing, the response techniques used to scale stimuli and subjects are less direct; usually the analyst must settle for weaker scale properties than are assumed under judgment methods.

Judgment methods

Judgment methods can be further classified into the subsets of (a) quantitative-judgment methods; and (b) variability methods. The subclasses indicate the *manner* in which the subject is asked to respond to the stimuli, in accord with some prespecified attribute. In the quantitative judgment procedure the subject attempts to make *direct* estimates of the relationships among the stimuli. As an illustration of this type of approach, assume that a housewife is presented with five types of chocolate bar of varying degrees of sweetness. The following types of instruction are illustrative of quantitative-judgment methods:

1. Rate each candy bar with regard to sweetness on a scale of five equal intervals.
2. Pick a number for the sweetness of candy bar *A*. Now assign

numbers to candy bars B through E which represent the relative degree of sweetness of each to the sweetness of bar A.
3. Determine whether the sweetness of candy bar B is closer to the sweetness of A than candy bar C is to the sweetness of A.
4. Given that candy bar A has a sweetness of 100, what is the sweetness of bars B through E?

As can be noted from these instructions, quantitative-judgment methods require a lot from the subject in terms of discriminatory ability (even though the subject is not asked for *her* preferred level of "sweetness"). Some techniques assume ratio scales on the psychological continuum (for example, instruction 1). In other instances (for example, instruction 3) the demands on the subject's ability are less stringent.

Variability methods make use of the "confusion" (or lack thereof) of a subject's judgments. The less variable (over subjects or over repeated stimuli for a given subject) the estimated comparative sweetness of, say, candy bar A versus B is, the greater the difference in scale values is assumed. The following types of instructions are illustrative of variability methods:

1. For all pairs of candy bars, $AB, AC,$ etc., which bar is the sweeter of each pair?
2. Place the candy bars in rank order with regard to sweetness.
3. Place the candy bars into three groupings, not necessarily equally spaced, according to sweetness.

Variability methods typically are used in the construction of interval scales. Illustrations of this class of techniques are the procedures based on "just noticeable differences" and Thurstone's law of comparative judgment. We shall discuss some applications of these procedures later.

Response methods

Most response methods where an attempt is made to scale *both* stimuli and subjects lead to "weaker" (usually only ordinal) scales than are obtained from judgment methods. The preferences expressed by the subject are assumed to be affected by *both* the stimulus and the subject's attitude about the characteristic being scaled. Most applications of response methods, for example, scalograms, summated scales, are undertaken to see if some content of interest, say, "consumer attitudes toward big business" is scalable in the sense that a subject's response to a particular statement (her agreement or disagreement with the statement) can be predicted from her overall rank order among respondents with regard to *all* statements in the questionnaire.

Applications of Scaling Techniques

Market researchers and others interested in attitude measurement have applied many of the techniques of behavioral scaling and have used a variety of specific scales. We shall comment on the principal scaling procedures in terms of assumption structure and mechanics of construction and then indicate some illustrative applications.

Thurstone's comparative judgment technique

Thurstone's law of comparative judgment represents one of the better known techniques of eliciting interval (or sometimes ratio) scales by variability methods. As discussed earlier, scale values are based on the degree of "confusion" evinced over a group of subjects or over replications of the stimuli for a single subject. If a large (for example, 95 per cent) proportion of a group prefer item *A* to item *B,* the technique assumes that the scale distance between *A* and *B* is "greater" than if a small (for example, 55 per cent) proportion of a group prefer *A* to *B.*

Thurstone reports an application of the procedure to the determination of the "values" assigned to a set of five birthday gifts [171]:

> *A* — a leather brief case
> *B* — a large dictionary
> *C* — a portable record player
> *D* — a desk lamp
> *E* — a pen and pencil set

Subjects (college students) were asked to state the preference for a specific item (say, the receipt of gift *A* versus *B*) for all possible pairs of items. The subject was then given comparisons to make of the type *AB* versus *C* in which a choice had to be made between receiving a single item and a pair of items. Finally the subject was asked to choose between two-item combinations of the type *AB* versus *CD*. The total possible combinations were as follows:

Single-pair comparisons	10
Single-double comparisons	30
Double-double comparisons	15
	55

Thurstone then tabulated the proportion of preferences for a total of 194 subjects. One version of the technique of deriving scale differences from proportions is based on the following assumptions:

1. The subjects can preferentially order all stimuli.
2. The distribution of subjective values associated with a given stimulus is in accord with the normal distribution (bell-shaped) with common variance over all pairs and equal correlations among pairs.

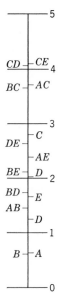

Fig. 2.3 Thurstone Scale—Gift Items. Reproduced, with permission, from L. L. Thurstone, *The Measurement of Values* (Chicago: University of Chicago Press), 1959, p. 208.

The results of the analysis are shown in Fig. 2.3. In this particular application Thurstone was able to obtain a ratio scale. It is interesting to note that item *C,* the record player, received a subjective value of more than four times that of item *B,* the dictionary, despite the fact that the prices of the two items were approximately equal. In this specific study it also turned out that the additivity of subjective values held. That is, the subjective value of a combination of two items was approximately equal to the sum of the subjective values of the two items taken singly.

In most applications of Thurstone's comparative judgment technique only interval scales are sought. Also, in many types of application it is probable that the additivity assumption does not hold; as Thurstone points out, the subjective value of a pair of shoes is more than twice the value of a right shoe when the left one has been lost.

Although there have been relatively few reported applications of Thurstone's comparative judgment technique to marketing problems, Benson [21] has discussed the successful use of this procedure (and various modifications) in scaling consumer preferences. It is likely that more applications will be undertaken as familiarity with its potential is gained by marketing researchers. Day [52] has used the method of paired comparisons to simulate distributions of consumer preferences.

Guttman's scaling technique

The Guttman scaling procedure is an illustration of a response procedure in which the analyst's intention is to scale both stimuli and subjects. For the most part, an ordinal scale is as strong a measure as can be obtained by this technique. Guttman [94] reports an application of the technique in determining whether a group of students possessed a scalable attitude toward a certain textbook, *A Nation of Nations,* by Louis Adamic. A questionnaire containing seven statements about the book was devised and administered to fifty students.

Figure 2.4 shows the questionnaire, and Fig. 2.5 illustrates the results of the first trial undertaken to determine whether the sample items are scalable. A total score for each subject is obtained by adding the weights shown beside each response in Fig. 2.4. The left-hand column of Fig. 2.5 shows the array of total scores. The

A Nation of Nations

1. *A Nation of Nations* does a good job of analyzing the ethnic groups in this country.

    _____Strongly agree(4)   _____Agree(3)   _____Undecided(2)
    _____Disagree(1)   _____Strongly disagree(0)

2. On the whole, *A Nation of Nations* is not as good as most college text-books.

    _____Strongly agree(0)   _____Agree(1)   _____Undecided(2)
    _____Disagree(3)   _____Strongly disagree(4)

3. Adamic organizes and presents his material very well.

    _____Strongly agree(4)   _____Agree(3)   _____Undecided(2)
    _____Disagree(1)   _____Strongly disagree(0)

4. As a sociological treatise, Adamic's book does not rate very high.

    _____Strongly agree(0)   _____Agree(1)   _____Undecided(2)
    _____Disagree(3)   _____Strongly disagree(4)

5. Adamic does not discuss any one group in sufficient detail so that a student can obtain a real insight into problems of ethnic group relations in this country.

    _____Strongly agree(0)   _____Agree(1)   _____Undecided(2)
    _____Disagree(3)   _____Strongly disagree(4)

6. By providing a panorama of various groups, *A Nation of Nations* lets the student get a good perspective on ethnic group relations in this country.

    _____Strongly agree(4)   _____Agree(3)   _____Undecided(2)
    _____Disagree(1)   _____Strongly disagree(0)

7. *A Nation of Nations* is good enough to be kept as a textbook for this course.

    _____Strongly agree(4)   _____Agree(3)   _____Undecided(2)
    _____Disagree(1)   _____Strongly disagree(0)

Fig. 2.4 Questionnaire: Guttman scaling technique for novel, *A Nation of Nations*. Reproduced, with permission, from L. Guttman, "Measuring the True State of Opinion," in *Motivation and Market Behavior,* R. Ferber and H. Wales (eds.) (Homewood, Ill.: Richard D. Irwin, 1958), p. 297.

remaining columns show the response of each person to each statement. For example, the subject who evinced a total score of 28, answered "strongly agree" on statement 1 and received a score of 4. (This individual checked the response weighted 4 for all seven statements.)

The search for scalability requires that the data exhibit a particular type of pattern. For example, in statement 1, if the response weighted 4 is higher than 3, etc., the nine people in category 4 for statement 1 should be the top nine people. As it turns out (Fig. 2.5) we note that only six of the nine are in the top nine, overall.

Score	1 (4 3 2 1 0)	2 (4 3 2 1 0)	3 (4 3 2 1 0)	4 (4 3 2 1 0)	5 (4 3 2 1 0)	6 (4 3 2 1 0)	7 (4 3 2 1 0)
28	X	X	X X	X	X	X	X
25	X	X	X X	X	X	X X	X
25	X	X	X X	X	X	X	X
24	X	X X	X X	X	X	X	X
23	X	X	X	X X	X	X X	X
23	X	X X	X	X	X	X	X
23	X	X X	X	X	X	X	X
22	X	X	X	X	X	X	X
21	X	X	X	X	X	X	X
21		X	X	X	X	X	X
21		X	X	X	X	X	X
21	X	X	X	X	X X	X	X
21	X	X	X	X	X	X X	X
20	X	X	X	X	X	X	X X
20	X	X X	X	X	X X	X	X
20	X	X	X	X	X	X X	X
20	X	X	X	X	X	X X	X
19	X	X	X	X	X	X	X
19	X	X	X	X	X	X	X
18	X	X	X	X	X	X	X
18	X	X	X	X	X X	X	X
18	X	X	X	X X	X	X	X
18	X	X	X	X	X X	X	X
17	X	X	X	X	X	X	X
17	X	X X	X	X	X	X X	X
16	X	X X	X	X	X	X	X
16	X	X	X	X	X	X	X
16	X	X	X X	X	X	X	X X
16	X	X	X	X X	X	X	X X
15	X X	X	X	X	X	X	X
15	X	X	X	X X	X	X X	X
15	X	X	X	X	X X	X	X X
15	X	X	X X	X	X	X	X
14	X X	X	X X	X	X	X	X
14	X	X	X	X X	X	X	X
13	X X	X X	X	X	X	X X	X
13	X	X X	X	X X	X	X	X X
12	X X	X	X X	X	X	X X	X X
12	X	X X	X X	X	X	X X	X X
11	X	X	X	X	X	X X	X
11	X	X	X	X X	X	X X	X
10	X	X	X	X	X	X X	X
9	X	X X	X	X	X	X X	X X
8	X	X X	X	X	X	X	X X
7	X	X X	X X	X	X X	X	X
7	X	X	X X	X X	X	X	X
7	X	X	X X	X	X	X	X
6	X	X	X X	X X	X	X	X
5	X	X X	X X	X	X X	X	X X
4		X	X	X	X	X	X
Freq.	9 27 2 12 0	8 24 0 13 5	10 25 8 7 0	3 7 16 14 10	3 14 5 21 7	9 21 7 12 1	11 19 5 11 4

Fig. 2.5 First trial for content scale: *A Nation of Nations*. Reproduced, with permission, from L. Guttman, "Measuring the True State of Opinion," in *Motivation and Market Behavior*, R. Ferber and H. Wales (eds.) (Homewood, Ill.: Richard D. Irwin, 1958), p. 298.

If the content and subjects could be scaled perfectly, the x's would form a pattern like that shown in Fig. 2.6.

Guttman provides procedures for "adjusting and rearranging responses in order to see if subjects and/or content are scalable." Like the Thurstone comparative judgment technique, however, there have been few reported applications of Guttman scalogram analysis to marketing research. One application by Richards [146] describes a case in which Guttman scaling was successfully used to derive consumer attitudes regarding three mechanically different

Score	1					2					3					4					5					6					7				
	4	3	2	1	0	4	3	2	1	0	4	3	2	1	0	4	3	2	1	0	4	3	2	1	0	4	3	2	1	0	4	3	2	1	0
28	x					x					x					x					x					x					x				
25	x					x					x					x					x						x						x		
25	x					x					x					x					x					x								x	
24	x					x					x					x					x					x									x
23	x					x					x					x					x						x								x
23	x					x					x					x					x						x								x
23	x					x					x					x					x						x								x
22	x					x					x					x					x							x							x
21	x					x					x					x					x								x						x
· · · · ·																																			

Fig. 2.6 Characteristics of content scale under "ideal" conditions.

49

ballpoint pens. As more familiarity with these procedures is gained, it is to be expected that additional marketing research applications will appear in the literature.

The semantic differential scale

One of the most popular scaling techniques in marketing research is the semantic differential technique as developed by Osgood [141] and his associates. This procedure is simple to administer and enables the analyst to probe attitudes regarding both content and intensity to such stimuli as corporate names and brand names. Much of the work in "corporate image measurement" has utilized this technique.

This procedure is implemented by showing the respondent a set of bipolar adjectives, as, for example,

> powerful . . . . . . weak
> aggressive . . . . . passive
> honest . . . . dishonest

Each adjective pair is (usually) separated by continuum on which are marked off seven equal steps, with the following descriptors:

> Extremely _____
> Very _____
> Slightly _____
> Both _____ and _____
> Slightly _____
> Very _____
> Extremely _____

For each adjective pair the respondent is asked to score his attitude about the stimulus (for example, corporate name) by checking the appropriate intensity interval for each adjective pair. By summing over subjects a "profile" of the stimulus can be obtained. Moreover, by performing factor analyses (described in Chapter 3), the stimulus can be located in a multidimensional "semantic space" in which the axes of the space are orthogonal (that is, mutually perpendicular).

An interesting marketing application of the technique is reported by Eastlack [61]. Figure 2.7 shows the adjective pairs that Eastlack used (along a 9-point scale) for determining preferences

Lighter appearance in the cup	1 2 3 4 ☐ ☐ ☐ ☐	5 ☐	6 7 8 9 ☐ ☐ ☐ ☐	Darker appearance in the cup
Flavor of a weaker blend	☐ ☐ ☐ ☐	☐	☐ ☐ ☐ ☐	Flavor of a stronger blend
Less bitterness	☐ ☐ ☐ ☐	☐	☐ ☐ ☐ ☐	More bitterness
Less aroma in the cup	☐ ☐ ☐ ☐	☐	☐ ☐ ☐ ☐	More aroma in the cup
A less roasted flavor in the cup	☐ ☐ ☐ ☐	☐	☐ ☐ ☐ ☐	A more roasted flavor in the cup
Lighter body	☐ ☐ ☐ ☐	☐	☐ ☐ ☐ ☐	Heavier body
Poorer flavor in the cup	☐ ☐ ☐ ☐	☐	☐ ☐ ☐ ☐	Better flavor in the cup
Lighter color of grounds in the can	☐ ☐ ☐ ☐	☐	☐ ☐ ☐ ☐	Darker color of grounds in the can

(Center column label: The brand of coffee I prefer to use — The brand of coffee I prefer to use)

Fig. 2.7 Semantic differential coffee scale. Reproduced, with permission, from J. L. Eastlack, "Consumer Flavor Preference Factors in Food Product Design," *Journal of Marketing Research,* **1** (February 1964), pp. 38–42.

for eight characteristics of ground coffee blends. The purpose of the study was to determine the appropriate characteristics a new coffee blend should possess to appeal to a large segment of the population in a major regional market.

Figure 2.8 shows how the experimental blend (blend 3) compared with the market leaders (blends 1 and 2) for two of the characteristics: "appearance in the cup" and "bitterness." Compared with blends 1 and 2, blend 3 showed up lighter in appearance and less bitter. By comparing the position of blend 3 with the two "standard" blends, according to various appearance and flavor characteristics, the analyst was able to provide guidance for making product modifications in the experimental blend.

Many applications of the semantic differential technique have been made to marketing research problems. In the measurement of corporate image by this technique, studies have been reported by several researchers [35, 138, 161]. Crespi [48] discusses its use in the development of styling images for appliance designs.

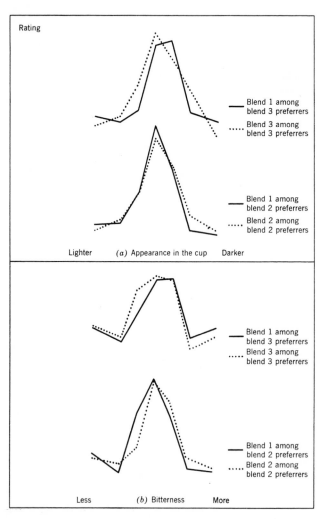

Fig. 2.8 *(Left)* Distribution of ratings of different blends by appearance in the cup and by bitterness. *(Right)* Comparison of blend ratings by different preferring groups for appearance in the cup and for bitterness. Reproduced, with permission, from J. L. Eastlack, "Consumer Flavor Preference Factors in Food Product Design," *Journal of Marketing Research,* **1** (February 1964), pp. 38–42.

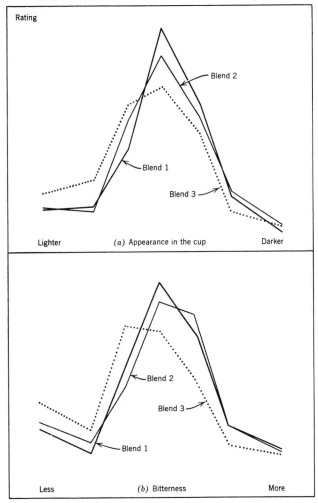

Fig. 2.8   (*continued*)

These references are only illustrative of the wide application that has been made of the semantic differential technique.

Other types of scaling procedures

The foregoing illustrations hardly exhaust the types of scale that have been designed and utilized by behavioral scientists and, more recently, by marketing researchers. We consider, briefly, two other types of scale.

Rating scales

A common measurement technique consists of rating scales in which the respondent rates her reaction to certain stimuli on a series of equal-appearing intervals, ranging from "extreme like" to "extreme dislike." Harris [98] has reported an application in which responses on a 21-point rating scale were used to "predict" sales of various patterns of dinnerware. Harris constructed preference indexes for each of ten fine china patterns and each of nine earthenware patterns by computing the percentage of total (140) respondents who rated the design in the top three scale positions of the 21-point scale. He then correlated the preference index of each pattern with an index based on actual sales data of each pattern during the preceding 6-month period.

Figure 2.9 shows the relationship between attitudinal and sales indexes for the ten fine chinaware patterns. As can be noted, the agreement is good. Harris indicates that the method is being applied on a national basis with good predictive results.

The Q-sort technique

The objective of the Q-sort procedure developed by Stephenson [165] is to compare individuals rather than to develop scale values. Typically the subject is given a large number (75–150) of items and is asked to place them in eleven piles from "most favorable" to "least favorable" in terms of his preferences; usually some preassigned number must be placed in each pile. Each pile is given a score value. Each subject thus receives a score for each item. Based on their responses to each item, *subjects* can be grouped into clusters with regard to their similarity in response.

An illustration of the Q-technique has been reported by Banks and Gregg [13] where 68 measurements were *already* available for a group of 155 independent nations (that is, the preliminary Q-sort was not required). The purpose of the study was to see if there existed specific clusters of countries according to certain sets of political characteristics. The authors were able to identify five major factors that accounted for the groupings: (a) polarchy, consisting of economically developed western nations; (b) elitist,

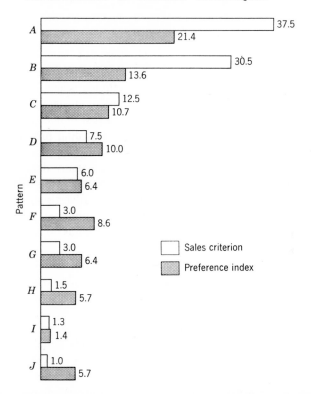

Fig. 2.9 Relation between preference index and sales criterion for 10 fine china patterns (N = 140). Reproduced, with permission, from D. Harris, "Predicting Consumer Reactions to Product Designs," *Journal of Advertising Research,* **4** (June 1964), pp. 34–37.

mostly made up of rapidly emerging African nations; (c) centrist, composed largely of the Communist states; (d) personalist, composed largely of Latin-American states, and (e) traditional, composed of such nations as Afghanistan, Ethiopia, and Libya.

It is not difficult to imagine parallels to this approach in marketing research. For example, clusters of consumers of various food items might be found which, in turn, are related to such variables as age, income, and dietary and caloric needs. Establishment of these segments would enable the marketing researcher to gear product and promotional strategy to these differentiated markets on a tailor-made basis.

The Limitations of Scaling Techniques

Our coverage of various scaling techniques has been, by necessity, limited. As we have noted, with the exception of the semantic differential and rating scales, the use of attitude scales in marketing research is still in its infancy. This limitation stems from more than just lack of familiarity of marketing researchers with scaling techniques. Several cautions in the use of scaling procedures are in order.

As Selltiz et al. [153] point out there are many dangers in the indiscriminant use of scaling devices. One danger is the "halo" effect where if a stimulus (for example, an advertisement) is being rated according to several criteria, the judges may extend a rather generalized impression about the stimulus to all attributes being rated.

Another type of error is overestimation of desirable qualities and underestimation of undesirable ones. If the rater is rating other people, there is also an often-found tendency to rate others as he sees himself.

Although we have not discussed the topic of scale values in describing such techniques as the semantic differential and rating scales, it is apparent that there is some question whether the intervals are subjectively equal. (In many cases this subjective equality of intervals is assumed to justify later mathematical operations.)

Finally, the question of how many intervals to use requires comment. Although some rating scales are designed to yield as many as 17 or 21 intervals, it is questionable whether respondents can rate stimuli on such a detailed basis. Miller [137], in summarizing a variety of experiments dealing with people's ability to make absolute judgments, indicates that most persons can only identify about seven gradations of a specific stimulus. It is not surprising, then, that many rating procedures involve at most a 7-point scale.

Validity of psychological scales

One of the major problems in designing and using scales is establishing their validity, that is, their accuracy and relevance to the construct being measured. If interest lies only in making predictions (not in being able to explain the concept), fewer demands are placed on the need for conducting validity tests. Still, establishing the predictive efficacy of a scale presents problems in its own right.

Several procedures are available for testing scale validity. In some instances the researcher is interested merely in the "face" validity of the test items. Here experts in the field may be asked to judge the representativeness of the test items. In other instances the researcher may attempt to match the test against some external criterion (which frequently turns out to be another attitudinal test). Finally, the analyst may attempt to develop criteria for answering the question of *why* the scale predicts well. If so, he has attempted to test the validity of the *construct* underlying the test measure.

Reliability of psychological scales

In testing for reliability the researcher is interested in the extent to which the scale is free from experimental error and in the reproducibility of the test results over individuals and time. A common technique in testing for reliability is to split test items into subgroups (for example, even versus odd questions) and then to conduct correlation analyses among subgroups. Other procedures involve repeated application of the test to the same individual at separate points in time or giving the test to a group of respondents who are assumed to be alike (according to an external criterion) with respect to the attribute being measured.

Attempts to establish the validity and reliability of psychological scales and attitude tests are still subject to much difficulty and uncertainty as to the interpretation of results and their generalization over individuals and situations. More important from the marketing researcher's point of view, however, is the need to *translate* predictions from attitude scales and preference indexes into measures of *direct* interest to the manager. It is one thing to assign numbers to, say, the consumer desirability of various product characteristics; it is quite another to predict the sales that would be generated if product characteristics were changed in the suggested direction. What is it worth to the corporation to "improve" its image? Even if segments of the market can be identified according to personality characteristics, how does one design advertising copy or select advertising media to appeal to various segments of the market? What market segments should be sought by the firm in the development of its strategy? Unfortunately, even if meaningful attitude scales can be developed, it is not at all apparent in many instances what the implications of these measurements are for marketing policy.

Other Behavioral Research Techniques in Marketing

Our understanding of people's behavior — be they consumers, distributors, competitors, or fellow managers — is still fragmentary and uncertain. In this section we discuss what appear to be useful research vehicles for the development and test of hypotheses about human behavior. Although our main focus is on studies of consumer behavior, the same methods are applicable to the investigation of behavior in other contexts.

There are good reasons for emphasizing consumer behavior as an illustrative focus. Much of the work in market segmentation is based on assumed differences in people with regard to brand preferences, reception to advertising appeals, and so on. The design of new product introductions may be geared to some theory about "tastemakers" and their influence on the degree and speed of new product acceptance [154]. Advertising campaigns may be built around themes with special appeal for specific social classes [125]. The pricing relationships among different models of a product may be based, in part, on how consumers impute quality differences from price differences.

As in the earlier sections of the chapter, we shall concentrate on recently developed techniques and applications. Although no attempt will be made to cover all procedures that behavioral scientists have used, we hope to describe at least the principal ones of content analysis, sociogram analysis, and experimental gaming.

1. Content analysis

A large part of the marketer's task is concerned with communications or, as Crane [47] puts it, "who says what to whom in what settings, by which channels, and with what purposes and what effects." Content analysis represents a research technique for quantitatively describing the content of communication. The uses of content analysis are several. The technique may be used in the study of trends in the content of communication (for example, advertisements of a specific product class) or for making comparisons among communications at a given point in time. These comparisons may refer to the characteristics of the transmitter, the receiver, the communication channel, or all three.

There are no set procedures for conducting content analysis. One could count the number of words in each communication, the number of "affective" words, the number of themes, and so on. One could use attribute classification, ordinal scaling, or higher forms of scales. Communications could be summarized in terms of subject matter, origin of communication, destination of communication, direction of statement (for example, favorable or unfavorable regarding a specific issue), and intensity of statement.

Designing content analyses requires the establishment of "dictionaries" that contain operational definitions of terms which are to be used in the analysis of themes and images. As an illustration, Stone, Dunphy, and Bernstein [168] have listed a set of terms which was developed to classify product images and institutional images. This list is shown in Fig. 2.10.

To illustrate their approach, suppose we wished to determine the differences between Ford and Chevrolet advertisements with regard to product image. All words referring to "strength" (tough, durable, resistant, etc.) would be counted for each set of advertisements. Similarly, other descriptors in the product properties column of Fig. 2.10 would be checked and appropriate frequencies tabulated. The resulting frequency counts for Ford versus Chevrolet advertisements could be contrasted and inferences drawn regarding theme, intended audience, and the extent to which various types of appeals are used.

Harvey [99] has reported an interesting application of content analysis as used in the prediction of the characteristics that discriminate between best-selling versus poor-selling novels. Harvey analyzed a sample set of novels in terms of such variables as: (a) change or movement in the plot; (b) amount and kind of emotion expressed in the story; (c) personalities of major characters; and (d) simplicity of style. Some 22 pairs (each composed of a best-selling and poor-selling novel) constituted the total sample. Some 100 to 150 hours were required to analyze each book. Harvey found that the best-selling novels (compared to poor-selling novels) showed the following:

Product Properties	*Institutional References*
Strength	Roles
Versatility	Organization
Economy	Management
Reliability	Finance
Appearance	Marketing
Total Assets	Consumption
Weakness	Scientific
Expense	Technological
Total Liabilities	*Product Areas*
Quantity	Transportation
Many — large	Domestic
Few — small	Education
Metrics	Defense
Relational	Engineering
Total Quantity	*Materials*
High Rate	*Components*
Low Rate	*Actions*
Change	Need
Increase	Use
Decrease	Facilitate
Stasis	Communicate
Transform	Process
Total Change	Stress
Sum Decline	*Logic*
Sum Improve	Cause
Time	Not
Past	*Style*
Present	Emphasis
Future	Underemphasis
Unit	Emotional
Total Time	*Evaluation*
	Good
	Bad

Fig. 2.10 "Dictionary" of content terms. Reproduced, with permission, from P. J. Stone, D. C. Dunphy, and A. Bernstein, "Content Analysis Applications at Simulmatics," *The American Behavioral Scientist,* **8** (May, 1965), pp. 16–18.

1. More emotion in terms of sentimentality, sensationalism, and the central male character's affection for other characters in the plot.
2. Certain style variables such as readability and wordage.

Harvey then went on to develop predictive formulas using a

discriminant analysis (see Chapter 3). He found statistically significant differences between the characteristics of best-selling and poor-selling novels that could be used to assist editors in forecasting sales for new manuscripts.

Sociogram analysis

Still another behavioral technique, sociogram analysis, shows some promise for assisting the marketing researcher. The objective of sociogram analysis is to portray communications networks in interacting systems.

Coleman, Menzel, and Katz [38] were interested in studying the social processes by which new ethical drugs were tried and adopted. Was the rate of adoption associated with the behavior of so-called "opinion leaders" (those prestigious physicians whose decision to adopt the new drug was emulated by "follower" physicians)? The authors asked, among other questions, "Who are the three or four physicians with whom you most often find yourself *discussing cases* or therapy in the course of an ordinary week — last week, for instance?"

Figure 2.11 shows a portion of the network which the authors were able to develop from replies to this question. Each circle represents a physician; arrows indicate the direction of the relationship. For example, an arrow from 04 to 05 indicates that Dr. 04 names Dr. 05 as one of his most frequent discussants. Double-headed arrows indicate a mutual naming by each physician. As noted from the chart, Dr. 31 was named by seven different colleagues. Dr. 30, on the other hand, is an isolated physician in terms of this group; he neither names nor is named by other physicians in the group.

In this problem one could develop from the sociogram groups of "integrated" and "isolated" doctors and study the rate of adoption for each group. Coleman, Menzel, and Katz did essentially this and noted that *integrated physicians generally adopted the new drug before the group of isolated physicians.*

Sociograms thus represent a convenient means for describing interrelationships among components of a behavior system and can give some insight into social interactions regarding the diffusion of innovation, message transmission, influence-relationships, and the like. Although their use in marketing is still at an early

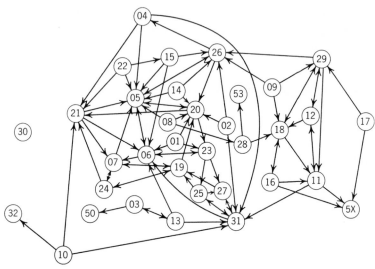

Fig. 2.11 Physician discussion network. Reproduced, with permission, from J. Coleman, H. Menzel, and E. Katz, "Social Processes in Physicians' Adoption of a New Drug," in *Quantitative Techniques in Marketing Analysis*, R. E. Frank, A. A. Kuehn and W. F. Massy, (eds.) (Homewood, Ill.: Richard D. Irwin, 1962), pp. 239–264.

stage, it is probable that this technique will gain increasing application in future marketing research studies.

3. Experimental gaming

Marketing research practitioners are also beginning to use a popular vehicle of the experimental psychologist, the experimental game. The central idea of experimental gaming involves the construction of a controlled environmental setting in which certain hypotheses about behavior can be tested. Although ideally we would like to perform experiments under field conditions, the complexity of real systems and the difficulty of control usually prohibit the conduct of full-scale experimentation.

Experimental games have been designed and conducted in a variety of contexts, for example, consumer choice (brand switching, store selection, reaction to price changes, information valuation), organizational behavior (conformity, information transmission), and competition (conflict and negotiation games).

One of the first attempts to apply experimental gaming techniques to the study of consumer behavior has been reported by Pessemier [142]. Pessemier designed a series of shopping trips in which subjects were given assortments of goods (toothpastes, toilet soaps) at various prices. A principal objective of the games was to see at what price differentials subjects would switch from their preferred brand to some less preferred brand. With regard to the "realism" of such experiments, Pessemier states:

"Since in the market it is often difficult to determine the demands or preferences for branded products over a moderate range of price variation, the question naturally arises: Can it be done in a controlled environment? An affirmative answer can be given *provided* the buyer can be placed in a position where the consequences of his actions in the experimental environment will have an impact on his well-being and conduct similar to what they would have in the market; the experimental conditions should be *psychologically equivalent* to the market, not necessarily physically identical. If the experimental situation is made 'real' by duplicating those aspects of the market which influence buyer action, then the experimental results will closely parallel the decisions made by consumers confronted by similar conditions in everyday life."

The results of Pessemier's experimental study indicated the following:

1. No significant differences in brand-switching behavior existed between male and female subjects.
2. Brand preference was more closely related to socioeconomic characteristics than to age characteristics.
3. As price continued to decline, the rate of brand switching tapered off.
4. Average brand loyalties differed over product classes and among brands within product class.

The implications of Pessemier's experiments for marketing management are interesting. To the extent to which experimental findings of this sort can be validated in the real world, methods are now becoming available for developing marketing "laboratories" where strategies can be pretested — at relatively low cost and risk — before being implemented in the actual market place.

Another interesting application of experimental gaming has been reported by Wells and Chinsky [182]. In this series of experiments the purpose was to study the effect of competing "messages" (spoken numbers) on respondent selection of a specific numeral after the sequence was completed. In one set of trials each number received an equal share of the total (randomized) message stream. Shares of the stream were then varied. Other variations of the experiment involved placing a block of the same number near the end of the sequence and presenting some blocks of the same number in "bursts" throughout the message stream. The authors found out that for a given share of the total sequence, the perceived "salience" of the message could be increased by using "bursts" of the same number over short intervals of the message sequence (as opposed to random placement in the message). Perceived salience could also be increased by increasing a given number's share of the total stream, but diminishing returns set in fairly quickly.

Although the foregoing experiment is "artificial," the implications for the development of advertising strategies — for example, advertising pulsing — are not trivial. Furthermore, as the authors suggest, the experimental technique can be made more realistic to include "content" in the message and by having subjects incur a cost for receiving additional messages.

Experimental gaming has also been used to study the behavior of brand-loyal versus brand-switching customers. Tucker [173] examined the development of brand loyalty under a set of controlled conditions in which all brands were virtually identical except for identifying symbols. He found that some consumers developed rather substantial loyalties, even where no discriminable differences existed among brands. A "rational" explanation of this behavior might be that such loyalty can be developed in the effort to avoid whatever psychological (or economic) costs the consumer ascribes to switching effort itself. In a more artificial set of conditions, this finding was substantiated and the experimenters were able to develop some additional findings on trying-rates and brand-switching characteristics associated with new product introduction [87].

Use of the experimental method in the study of consumer marketing is gaining momentum, and several experiments dealing with various aspects of consumer behavior under controlled conditions have been reported [31, 46, 104, 133]. Researchers have also explored, via experimental gaming, the nature of managerial decision behavior under uncertainty and the manner in which business executives acquire and use information [82, 88, 162].

Undoubtedly experimental methods in marketing research will continue to gain acceptance as more practitioners develop the necessary background and statistical skills for designing and analyzing data developed from experimental games. Although more work obviously needs to be undertaken in validating the results of controlled experiments under the ongoing conditions of the real market place, the possibilities for the development and test of basic hypotheses about buyer behavior, at the very least, are provocative.

The Current Status of Behavioral Research in Marketing

Previous sections of this chapter have described a variety of techniques — motivation research, attitude scales, content analysis, sociograms, experimental games — for measuring human behavior and testing hypotheses about buyer choice processes. To date, application of many of these techniques by marketers has been limited to "exploratory" studies. We believe that the use of many of these techniques developed by scholars in disciplines outside of marketing will expand as marketing researchers become more acquainted with their potential. Not that the techniques are without limitations. As was noted earlier, establishing the validity and reliability of attitude scales is no easy matter. Nevertheless, if verbalized responses under certain situations are predictive of behavior, the savings in research costs and time could be substantial.

Stefflre [164] has reported some interesting research aimed at bridging the gap between verbalized responses and actual choice behavior. Essentially Stefflre attempts to correlate verbalized responses regarding consumers' *perceptions* of various features of brands within a given product class with *actual behavior* derived from purchase data. His objective is to predict market share if various features of an existing brand are changed or if a new brand is introduced into the market. This type of approach — if substantiated over a variety of product classes — offers productive possibilities for product and package design and copy theme development.

Despite the plethora of techniques now available for measuring behavior, we still know very little with regard to behavioral *theory*. It is not that theories of buyer behavior do not exist; as a matter of fact, a major problem is to integrate the many models that have been proposed for "explaining" buyer behavior. As Kotler [115] points out, we already have several models of the buyer behavior process.

1. The Marshallian *economic man* who is presumably concerned with economic costs and benefits.
2. The Pavlovian *conditioned man* who is strongly influenced by habit and "reinforced" past behavior.
3. The Freudian *psychoanalytic man* whose choices are purportedly influenced by motivations deep within his unconscious.
4. The Veblenian *social-psychological man* whose choices are conditioned by cultural values and peer group behavior.
5. The Hobbesian *organizational man* whose behavior (for example, in the role of purchasing agent) is influenced by both individual and group (organizational) values.

Whereas in earlier sections of the chapter we have discussed various techniques — motivation research, psychophysics, sociogram analysis, the semantic differential — for dealing with various aspects of the foregoing models, we have not discussed choice theory, as such. This has been by design; nothing like universal agreement currently exists about *the* theory of buyer behavior. Possibly the buyer is some combination of all of these models or he reflects each model, conditional upon the situation involved. In any event, progress to date in "explaining" behavior has appeared to lag behind the development of techniques for measuring this behavior.

It is our hope that more effort will be expended on the development and test of behavioral theory; in particular, the conditions under which each proposed model holds. For the long run increasingly sophisticated measurement techniques will still be severely limited if commensurate theory is not developed. As discussed earlier, experimental gaming procedures would appear to provide a useful vehicle for the development and test of such theory, and of late this approach is receiving increasing attention.

Summary

In this chapter we have attempted to introduce the reader to recent developments in attitude scaling and behavioral science techniques. We first discussed the managerial implications of buyer behavior and then described the nature of early efforts in this field, as classed under the generic label, "motivation research." Our attention then turned to the formal properties of measurement and the types of scales with which the behavioral scientist works.

We then discussed scaling techniques in terms of assumption structure and derivation procedures. This was followed by a brief description of specific scaling techniques, such as the semantic differential, rating scales, and the Q-technique. Various applications of these tools were briefly described, followed by a discussion of some of the problems of establishing scale validity and reliability.

Other behavioral procedures — content analysis, sociograms, and experimental gaming — were discussed and illustrated by applications. Finally, we discussed briefly some of the theories proposed for "explaining" buyer behavior and the need for additional research toward extending theoretical developments in this area. We expect that future behavioral research in marketing will encompass both attitudinal scaling and experimental gaming approaches.

3 The Application of Multivariate Statistical Techniques to Marketing Problems

Introduction

The analysis of complex marketing problems is gradually moving in the direction of increased reliance on an extensive array of statistical techniques. The use of statistics is not new to marketing research; probability sampling procedures are widely accepted in practice. The use of statistical techniques, however, as the basis for the analysis of results, as opposed to the design of the data collection process, is only just beginning. Exotic sounding terms such as "latin square," "factorial analysis," and "multiple regression and discriminant analysis," are slowly finding their way into the marketing literature.

Regardless of the labels given to each of these techniques, many have one important characteristic in common, namely, they are *multivariate statistical procedures;* that is, they are procedures for simultaneously examining the relationship between some criterion of interest and any number of predictors. This is an extremely important characteristic for two reasons:

1. Most marketing problems require the evaluation of the interrelationships among large numbers of variables.
2. Until recently, constraints on the state of technology in marketing research made it virtually impossible to use simultaneous statistical procedures to assess the relationships between more than three or four variables at a time.

The number of calculations required by these procedures far outstrips the capacity of most clerical staffs. Even if this were not a problem, the likelihood of human error associated with performing large numbers of calculations is great. The advent of modern large-scale computers has removed this obstacle.

In addition, most of the multivariate statistical procedures have been programmed in a fashion that permits their use by individuals with a wide range of problems. The University of California at Los Angeles has developed a set of programs [55] capable of performing the calculations required by every one of the techniques discussed in this chapter (as well as many others). Other statistical packages have been developed at Harvard [42] and Princeton [27]. Few if any firms lack access to these computational resources or their equivalent.

The objectives of this chapter are to describe some of the more important multivariate techniques and to illustrate their application to marketing problems. The techniques discussed fall into two major categories: experimental and observational (nonexperimental) procedures. We first discuss the differences between the techniques that fall into each of these two groups. This is followed by a review of some of the principal types of experimental designs and their applications to such marketing problem areas as product policy and advertising. Our discussion of experimentation concludes with a review of some of the principal limitations of experimental procedures as applied to marketing problems.

The discussion of nonexperimental procedures focuses primarily on the logic underlying the various techniques and the types of problems to which they have been thus far applied. The chapter concludes with a brief section appraising the current state of application of multivariate techniques in marketing.

Experimental versus Nonexperimental Techniques

In the context of this chapter experiments are defined as studies in which implementation involves intervention by the observer beyond that required for measurement, whereas nonexperimental studies involve only that degree of intervention required for measurement.

Suppose we wanted to determine the effect of window displays on apple sales in supermarkets. We could for a given week, for each store in a chain, collect a record of the dollar value of apple sales per transaction together with a record of whether or not special window displays were used during the week. A comparison could then be made of stores with and without special displays to see if their average sales levels differ. Thus far our example has been based on the use of nonexperimental data.

We could change this to an experiment by requiring all the store managers to use displays during some specified period of time. Our experiment could then be used to measure the effect of the displays in terms of the change in apple sales per transaction from the week prior to the intervention to the time of the intervention. This form of experimentation is often called a "tryout."

Our tryout still leaves us with a rather serious problem of interpretation. To what extent would sales have changed from week to week had there been no window displays? To get around this difficulty we could divide our stores into two groups. One group would use displays while the other would continue as they had been. This second group is usually called a *control group.*

Given the division of stores into control and test groups, we could then introduce window displays into the test group. Suppose sales double in the test group? What are the implications of this change? Is it a valid measure of the effect of window displays?

The answers to these questions depend on what happened to sales in the control group. If they remained unchanged, the change in the test group apparently is completely due to the effect of window displays. Suppose instead that both test and control groups had changed by the same magnitude. Then in spite of the change in the test group our best estimate of the effect of window displays would be zero.

By specifying what stores are to be included in the experimental and control groups, another source of possible error inherent in our nonexperimental study can be reduced. In the nonexperimental study, store managers were free to choose for themselves whether window displays were to be used. The sales increase in stores with window displays could be attributable to the ability of store managers to discern under what conditions window displays for apples will be effective. If the researcher's problem is to evaluate the use of window displays, he needs a method for dividing stores into experimental and control groups that will avoid the possible self-selection bias of managers. The principal techniques used for such grouping are randomization and blocking. Their major purpose is to help ensure that the different groups in the experiment are comparable before intervention, except for variations that can be predicted by chance.

The logic underlying the use of control groups, randomization, and blocking (matching) is discussed in detail in the following sections of this chapter. Suffice it to say for now that by the use of these techniques experimentation has a number of built-in safeguards against making erroneous inferences regarding the nature and magnitude of the relationship under investigation. Given the effectiveness of experiments in providing less ambiguous results, the reader may be tempted to ask: Why bother with nonexperimental research?

In spite of the methodological advantages inherent in experimental techniques, nonexperimental designs are by far the most frequently used basis for inferring the relationships among a set of variables. Three of the principal reasons for this fact are: (a) experiments are often economically unfeasible; (b) it is often difficult or else impossible to intervene in the desired fashion; and (c) the time required to design and conduct an experiment may exceed the time available before the results are needed.

An example of the first limitation would be a study of the effect of grocery store size on the size of its retail trading area. The cost of manipulating store size for the purpose of the experiment would be prohibitive. With respect to the second limitation, a study aimed at determining the effect of income on the likelihood of a household purchasing a Cadillac would need to be nonexperimental as it is impossible to assign households to different income levels.

There are three types of nonexperimental studies:

1. Time series analysis,
2. Cross-sectional studies (studies at point-in-time),
3. Studies that combine both time series and point-in-time analysis.

The development of sales forecasts typically involves the use of historical time series as a partial basis for predicting future sales. For example, if we were interested in forecasting annual beer consumption in the United States, historical time series of annual beer consumption, disposable income, the proportion of the population between the ages of, say, 18 and 44, and the consumption of competing beverages (wines and distilled spirits) might be used as the basis for the analysis.

In contrast, most consumer surveys would be classified as cross-sectional investigations. They typically involve interviewing a number of customers during a specified period of time and using the same questionnaire. Nothing in the process of interviewing the households is done deliberately to cause them to differ from one another in their responses to the questionnaire. The differences that are observed are presumably those that existed among customers before the time of measurement, hence, are not a function of the measurement process.

The best known application of a combined time series and cross-sectional analysis is the design of a consumer panel. A consumer panel involves interviewing the same individuals on two or more occasions. For example, the Market Research Corporation of America (MRCA) runs a consumer panel based on a national sample of approximately 7500 households. Each household fills out a weekly diary of its food and household purchases. The same households participate week after week. As in the preceding examples the data generated describes the historical purchasing behavior of each household. No attempt is made by MRCA to change the purchasing behavior of the participants (for example, by sending them a special 5¢ off coupon for a particular product). At any one point in time information is available on each of a large number of households. In addition, if an analysis of time series is wanted, they are also provided by the same measurement process.

The next section discusses experimental techniques for studying the relationships between two or more variables. This is followed by a section on nonexperimental techniques. The chapter concludes with an appraisal of the present state of application of multivariate statistical techniques to marketing problems.

Experimentation

Experimental designs vary primarily along two dimensions:

1. The extent to which randomization and blocking procedures are used as a basis for increasing precision.

2. The number of variables that are simultaneously manipulated by the experimenter.

We first discuss the principal types of experimental designs. Next follows a discussion of "convariance analysis" which is just beginning to be widely recognized as a technique for increasing the precision of an experiment beyond what one can normally accomplish through blocking. Covariance analysis can be used in conjunction with any type of experimental design. Thus it does not compete as an alternative form of experimentation but instead can be used as a complement to whatever is deemed the most appropriate experimental design in a given situation. Our discussion will conclude with a review of some of the principal limitations associated with the application of experimental procedures to marketing problems.

Types of experimentation
Five types of experimental designs are to be discussed.

1. Completely randomized designs
2. Randomized block designs
3. Latin square designs
4. Double change over designs
5. Factorial designs

The first four of these permit the experimenter to manipulate only one experimental variable at a time, whereas the fifth category, factorial designs, was created for the express purpose of simultaneously experimenting with two or more variables at once. The first four types vary primarily in the extent to which they contain built-in protective devices aimed at reducing the degree of statistical error apt to be associated with the final results. Although our discussion provides a systematic review of the major alternative experimental designs, space does not permit it to be all inclusive. Readers interested in a more detailed discussion of the planning of experiments should see Cox [44]. For a discussion of the appropriate statistical techniques to be applied in a given situation, see Banks [14, 16], Cochran and Cox [36], Federer [69], and/or Kempthorne [111]. Banks provides the least technical explanation of the statistical techniques involved, whereas

Kempthorne assumes considerable prior exposure to the literature of statistics.

Completely Randomized Designs. The simplest design is one in which the allocation of "treatments" to "subjects" is done by chance. The term treatment refers to the alternatives whose effects are to be measured. For example, they may be different levels of advertising expenditure, different levels of call per customer for a sales force, or different sizes or types of package designs. A subject (often called a test unit) is the individual, geographic unit, or organization whose response is being studied. For example, depending on the nature of the investigation, a test unit may be a sales territory, a metropolitan area, a retail store, or an individual customer.

The commonest application of completely randomized designs is the testing of direct mail advertising and the evaluation of advertisements using split-run procedures. The typical procedure followed in conducting these experiments is illustrated by a study of the effect of color on the response of individuals to direct mail advertising conducted by Dunlop [60]. Renewal notices were sent to the members of the Kansas State Alumni Association. The notices varied in only one respect, their color. Four different colors were used — yellow, blue, cherry, and white. The mailing list consisted of 572 names. Every fourth person on the list received the same color card. The first person chosen was selected randomly from the first four names on the list. This procedure (systematic random sampling) for allocating subjects to treatments (the different colored mailing pieces) constitutes one type of chance procedure for deciding which subject should receive which color mailing piece. The results of the experiment are reported in Table 3.1.

The design of most split-run experiments corresponds closely to that used in the aforementioned illustration. Usually a newspaper or a magazine prints two different advertisements in the same issue, on the same page, but in alternate copies. The papers are then distributed. The advertisements usually contain some type of an offer requiring the reader to respond by mail. The performance of the ads is then judged by comparing their response rates to the offer. The type of randomized design that we have just described is called an after-only design. The format of this design is shown in the following table:

	Experimental Groups			Control Group
	Yellow	Blue	Cherry	White
Prior selection	Yes	Yes	Yes	Yes
Before measurement	No	No	No	No
Treatment	Yes	Yes	Yes	"No"
Uncontrolled events	Yes	Yes	Yes	Yes
After measurement	Yes	Yes	Yes	Yes

Our color experiment had one "control group" — those individuals who received white cards. Prior selection by a chance mechanism was used to pick the individuals who received the cards in each of the four groups. There were three experimental groups, and different colored announcements were sent to each of them. Each of the four groups, however, was vulnerable to the effects of uncontrolled events. For example, if the mailings arrived during a peak vacation period there might be a lower rate of return. However, given that the mailings were sent at the same time, and, furthermore, that a chance mechanism was used to allocate subjects to treatments, then the expected decrease in response rate would be the same for all four of the groups, leaving undisturbed our ability to compare the *relative* responses to each treatment. The only measurement taken of each individual was after their exposure to the mailing (hence the term after-only).

Although this form of experimentation has the advantage of being quite simple to interpret, unfortunately in a wide range of research situations the results are not sufficiently reliable to be of much use. The differences in the response of one treatment versus

Table **3.1** The Number of Mailing Pieces Sent Out and Returned by Color

	White		Yellow		Blue		Cherry	
	Sent	Ret'd.	Sent	Ret'd.	Sent	Ret'd.	Sent	Ret'd.
	147	60	144	73	141	65	140	54
% Returned	40.8%		50.7%		46.1%		38.6%	

Source: Adapted with permission from J. William Dunlop, "The Effect of Color in Direct Mail Advertising," *Journal of Applied Psychology,* Vol. 34 (1950), p. 281.

another could easily be due to the effect of other variables. For example, suppose twenty grocery stores were randomly split into groups of ten stores each. Furthermore, suppose that a special type of display for apples was put in one group of ten stores and the other group continued to use their standard procedures. Suppose apple sales per store during the period of the experiment were $200 higher for the stores with the new type of display. So what! If by chance more large stores were assigned to the new display group, then the average sales of this group would be expected to be higher. There are numerous factors, such as store size, that might actually differ between the two groups of stores and which might in turn be correlated with apple sales. The more important these factors are as determinants of apple sales per store relative to the display technique, the less confident we will be of our final results.

Fortunately procedures have been developed for protecting against the effects of many of these extraneous factors. *Blocking* is one such device.

Randomized Block Designs. One of the common misconceptions about experimental designs is that all the test units used must be as nearly homogeneous as possible. Presumably, if the units were completely homogeneous, any differences obtained after the introduction of the experimental variable from one treatment to the next would be due to its effect and not to the influence of some other factor such as store size or degree of competition.

Fortunately complete homogeneity of test units is not a *requirement* for successful experimentation. If one or more of the sources of heterogeneity among test units can be identified, it may then be possible to stratify test units by this variable so that *within strata the test units are relatively homogeneous,* whereas there may be a large degree of heterogeneity among strata. For example, suppose we were interested in testing the effect of four different types of packaging on the sales of a perishable food product. A total of 96 test units are to be included in the experiment, each of which is an individual grocery store. One major source of heterogeneity among stores with regard to the sales of the product in question is store size. We could attempt to run the experiment with stores of the same size, but two problems would arise. First, there might not be a sufficient number of stores to permit this design to be implemented. Second, even if it could be done, we would be faced with the following question: Can the effect of a change in display on stores within a certain size range be generalized to stores outside that range?

One way around this problem is to use a *randomized block design*. In this design, the units are stratified (that is, the randomization is restricted) before treatments are allocated to the different test units (stores). For our illustration the random assignment of treatments is restricted to stores falling in a certain size range.

Table 3.2 illustrates one such design. The blocks in our illustration are three store sizes (small, medium, and large). Suppose each of these three blocks (or strata) were of equal size. This would imply that 32 stores would be assigned to each block.

Note that the allocation of stores to blocks would not be based on randomization. The stores would be deliberately assigned to each block on the basis of their size. Next the 32 stores within each block would be randomly assigned to each of the four treatment levels (*A, B, C,* or *D*), subject to the restriction that the four groups be equal in size. (Equal sample sizes for each block and within each block for each treatment, although they may simplify calculations a bit, are not necessary restrictions on the applicability of this type of design. The number of test units may be varied from block to block and treatment to treatment.)

This type of design has been used by the Schwerin Research Corporation as a basis for comparing the effects of alternative television commercials [151]. Schwerin invites people to a theater to see a program and a commercial. Prior to being exposed to them, the respondents fill out a questionnaire containing, in part, classification data (for example, socioeconomic characteristics, brand preferences for certain products) that will be subsequently used as a basis for *blocking* in the analysis of their responses. Next

Table **3.2** Hypothetical Randomized Block Design

Small stores	*A*	*B*	*C*	*D*
Medium stores	*A*	*B*	*C*	*D*
Large stores	*A*	*B*	*C*	*D*

the respondents are exposed to the program and the commercial. This is followed by questionnaires which record what they remember as well as their brand choices after exposure. Figure 3.1 illustrates one type of blocking procedure that they use. In effect, their pre-choice control factor amounts to blocking respondents on the basis of the brand they preferred prior to exposure. The figure also represents the result of the equivalent of one treatment (that is, the testing of one particular commercial). The design for testing alternative treatments would look schematically like Table 3.2 except that: (a) rather than block on stores they are blocking on brand preference before exposure to the commercial; (b) the treatments *A, B, C, D* are now alternative TV commercials rather than type of display; and (c) test units are now individuals instead of stores.

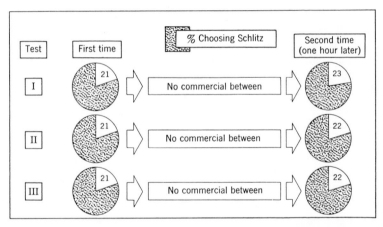

Fig. 3.1.   Consistency with no intervening stimulus. Reproduced, with permission, from Schwerin Research Corp., "Why TV Commercials Succeed," in R. E. Frank, A. A. Kuehn, and W. F. Massy, *Quantitative Techniques in Marketing Analysis* (Homewood, Ill.: Richard D. Irwin, 1962), pp. 166–176.

Blocking (or stratification) plays an important role in this and all subsequent designs we shall discuss. By blocking on a characteristic that is likely to be a major source of variation in the performance (for example, sales) of test units (for example, food stores), the units within each block are likely to be much more homogeneous. The greater this homogeneity the more precise will be the estimate of the effect of the experimental variable under study. Because of the many sources of variation among test units in the usual criterion of interest to marketing management (sales, market share), there is a need for some type of procedure for restricting randomization such as blocking.

In addition to the testing of TV commercials, randomized block designs have been applied to the study of alternative canned food display techniques [93] as well as to the study of merchandising practices for potatoes [119]. In most practical applications, however, the blocking techniques used are a bit more complex than those thus far described. The design that has received the most extensive application to marketing problems is the latin square, which is described in the following section.

Latin Square Designs. In the randomized block design discussed in the preceding section, an attempt is made to increase the degree of homogeneity among test units receiving different treatments by *blocking* on one variable so that all treatments must appear in a given block the same number of times. The latin square designs go one step further than this in that blocking is based on *two* variables at once in such a way that each treatment appears once within each stratum of each of the two bases for blocking. An illustration of this procedure is reported in Table 3.3. This type of design was used by Domenick to study the effect of various pricing, display, and packaging practices on apple sales in food stores [57].

Table **3.3** Schematic Layout of One of Domenick's Experiments

Day of Week	Store			
	1	2	3	4
Monday	*B*	*C*	*D*	*A*
Tuesday	*A*	*B*	*C*	*D*
Wednesday	*D*	*A*	*B*	*C*
Thursday	*C*	*D*	*A*	*B*

Source: Reproduced from B. A. Domenick, *Merchandising McIntosh Apples Under Controlled Conditions — Customer Reaction and Effect on Sales* (Unpublished Ph.D. Dissertation, Cornell University, 1952).

The test unit was a grocery store. There were four treatments (A, B, C, D). For example the treatments could be four different types of apple display. Stores and day of week are used as the two *blocking* variables. Treatment A was exposed to store 1 on Tuesday, store 2 on Wednesday, store 3 on Thursday and store 4 on Monday. Thus treatment A appeared once in each store and once on each day of the week. This is also true of treatments $B, C,$ and D.

The performance of treatment A (for example, average sales across the four A's) can be thought of as a weighted average, where the weights given to each store and day of the week are equal. Treatment B's performance is based on the same set of weights for stores and days of the week that were used to compute the performance of treatment A. This is also true for the weights used to compute the average performance of treatments C and D. In a design in which this was not done, variations in the weight given different days of the week or stores would be uncontrolled. By controlling this variation and insuring the comparability of the weights via the latin square, the researcher is usually able to increase the precision with which he can measure the effect of a given experimental variable.

For any number of treatments (say n) the latin square design requires n columns (stores) and n rows (days of the week) and therefore a minimum of n^2 observations. Usually a square is described in terms of the number of rows and columns it contains, such as 3 x 3 or 4 x 4, 5 x 5, etc. In practice it is rare that more than 5 x 5 or 6 x 6 is used.

Latin square designs have been applied to a wide range of marketing problems in widely varying circumstances. A number of applications have been focused on the problem of evaluating the effectiveness of advertising as well as other types of sales promotional tools. In addition to Domenick's work, several experiments have been conducted to evaluate various elements in the promotion of apples. Smith and Frye designed a latin square experiment to test the effect of color uniformity on apple sales [159]. They used a 3 x 3 design, which is reported in Table 3.4. The rows were three different stores, and columns consisted of three time periods. Three replications of the 3 x 3 design were included in the experiment, each consisting of a different set of three stores. Three

Table **3.4** Experimental Design and Apple Sales by Treatment, Nine Retail Food Stores, Atlanta, Georgia

	Experiment Period					
	Oct.–Nov. 11		Nov. 13–Nov. 28		Nov. 27–Dec. 9	
	Treat-ment*	Sales	Treat-ment*	Sales	Treat-ment*	Sales
First replication:						
Store 1	A	779	B	496	C	424
Store 2	B	312	C	314	A	238
Store 3	C	803	A	599	B	314
Second replication:						
Store 4	A	703	C	416	B	319
Store 5	B	376	A	458	C	276
Store 6	C	623	B	397	A	556
Third replication:						
Store 7	A	557	B	382	C	346
Store 8	B	313	C	489	A	396
Store 9	C	170	A	211	B	85

*Treatments represent color ranges of red delicious apples as follows: A, 75–100 per cent good red color; B, 50–75 per cent good red color; C, 50–100 per cent good red color.
Source: Reproduced from "How Color of Red Delicious Apples Affects Their Sales," Market Research Report–618 (U.S. Department of Agriculture, February 1964).

color ranges of red Delicious apples served on the treatments: treatment A — "highly colored," 75 to 100 per cent good red color; B — "partly red," 50 to 75 per cent good red color; and C — "combination," 50 to 100 per cent good red color (a mixture of treatment A and B test applies).

The results of the experiment indicated that customers most preferred the highly colored red apples and least preferred those in the partly red category. As a result, experiments are currently being conducted with electronic sorters to ascertain the feasibility of providing customers with more homogeneously color graded apples.

Table 3.5 presents another example in which a 2 x 2 latin square design was used by a Long Beach, California newspaper to study the impact of color advertisements on sales of jewelry,

Table **3.5**   Experimental Design Used in Studying Impact of Color Advertisements on Sales

Time Period	Jewelry Stores		Furniture Stores		Variety Stores	
	Store 1	Store 2	Store 1	Store 2	Store 1	Store 2
1	Color	B & W	Color	B & W	Color	B & W
2	B & W	Color	B & W	Color	B & W	Color

Source: Reproduced, with permission, from "Color Study Checks Sales in Stores," *Editor and Publisher* (June 13, 1959).

furniture, and variety stores [40]. The experiment consists of three 2 x 2 latin squares being run simultaneously.

Double Change-Over Designs. One of the most common devices for increasing the precision of an experiment is to expose each test unit to each treatment during consecutive time periods. This device is illustrated in Table 3.4 in which each of the nine stores included in the experiment was used in three consecutive time periods. By designing the experiment in this fashion the resulting differences in average sales for each treatment will not be due to any systematic differences in store size or characteristics. Thus one source of potential error has been removed.

Although this practice helps to solve one problem, however, it can contribute to the creation of another. Suppose the first treatment (A) administered to store 1 is quite effective. It might lead customers to stock up on apples which could lead to a lower level of performance for treatment B in the following period. In a sense B's performance would be artificially depressed. It would be lower than might be expected if, in fact, it was used outside the experimental context, because its observed effect in the experiment includes the negative *carry-over* effect of treatment A, which preceded it.

We could attempt to avoid this problem by lengthening the time period during which each treatment is exposed to a given test unit and/or by placing "rest periods" between treatments. In many situations, however, it is often necessary to use relatively short time periods, especially when individuals (such as store managers) are asked to deviate in some fashion from their normal procedures.

Table **3.6** Change-Over Design

		Store					
		1	2	3	4	5	6
Time	1	A	B	C	A	B	C
Period	2	B	C	A	C	A	B
	3	C	A	B	B	C	A

Fortunately it is possible to modify the latin square to overcome this problem. The change-over design permits the calculation of the carry-over effects. Table 3.6, which consists of a pair of 3 x 3 latin squares, presents an example of one such design.

Why two latin squares? Suppose only the first one were used. Could we ascertain the carry-over effect of, say, treatments A and B on C? Treatment C is always immediately preceded in time by B. For estimating the carry-over effects over two time periods, the only data we have for C is when A is two periods removed. If we are to have data capable of measuring the carry-over effect of A and B with respect to C we need to have measures of the other two conditions, namely, (a) when A immediately precedes C; and (b) when B is two periods removed from C.

Now let us look at the second latin square. This square was deliberately chosen so that it would fulfill both of these needs. The same logic can be used for justifying the need for the second square in the case of the carry-over effect of A and C on B and B and C on A.

Table 3.7 presents an actual application of this design [100]. The American Sheep Producers Council asked the Economics Research Service of the United States Department of Agriculture to help them test their current promotional program for retail lamb sales against two alternatives. Their current program used media advertising and merchandising, whereas the two alternatives they desired to test were (a) the use of a cooperative advertising program; and (b) no advertising or promotion of any kind of lamb.

Six-week time periods were chosen so as to permit enough time for the Council to promote its regular and cooperative advertising programs and for the retailer to respond to them. Six cities were chosen. Three were in the Northeast, which is a relatively high

Table **3.7** Double Change-Over Experimental Design Used in Lamb Promotion Study, 78 Supermarkets in 3 Midwestern and 3 Northeastern Cities, Three 6-Week Time Periods, September 1960 Through February 1961

Six-week time periods	Midwestern cities (Square I)			Northeastern cities (Square II)		
	St. Louis, Mo.	Omaha, Neb.	Des Moines, Iowa	Philadelphia, Pa.	Syracuse, N. Y.	Springfield-Holyoke, Mass.
September 6 through October 15	(A) Regular promotion	(B) Cooperative advertising	(C) No sponsored promotion	(A) Regular promotion	(B) Cooperative advertising	(C) No sponsored promotion
October 17 through November 26	(B) Cooperative advertising	(C) No sponsored promotion	(A) Regular promotion	(C) No sponsored promotion	(A) Regular promotion	(B) Cooperative advertising
Holiday season omitted						
January 2 through February 11	(C) No sponsored promotion	(A) Regular promotion	(B) Cooperative advertising	(B) Cooperative advertising	(C) No sponsored promotion	(A) Regular promotion

Source: Reproduced from "Promotional Programs for Lamb and Their Effects on Sales," Market Research Report–522 (U.S. Department of Agriculture, January 1962).

lamb-consuming area, and three were in the Midwest, a relatively low lamb-consuming area. In each city a panel of self-service food stores was randomly chosen for auditing lamb and other red meat sales. The holiday season was skipped because of competition of poultry, especially turkey, during this period.

The design was quite useful. It revealed that sales during periods of cooperative advertising were 26 per cent higher than those in which no promotion was done, whereas the Council's regular promotion resulted in only a 10 per cent differential.

An experiment similar in design to that of the Council was done for the American Dairy Association to study the effect of varying promotion on milk sales and on the sales of other dairy products [105]. In addition, a carry-over design has been used to study the effect of different promotional programs on apples sales in supermarkets [101].

Factorial Designs. So far our discussion has concentrated on experimental designs in which the effect of experimentally manipulating only one variable at a time was measured. One of the more common misconceptions about experimentation is that only one variable at a time can be manipulated. Fortunately this is not true. There are a number of designs capable of measuring the effects of more than one variable at a time. They are referred to as factorial designs.

For example, an experiment was performed on the effect of varying flavor intensity and sugar content on customer preferences for a soft drink [132]. A schematic presentation of the design is reported in Table 3.8.

Table **3.8** Soft Drink Factorial Design

		Sugar Content			
		1	2	3	4
Flavor	1.	*a*	*b*	*c*	*d*
intensity	2.	*e*	*f*	*g*	*h*
	3.	*i*	*j*	*k*	*l*
	4.	*m*	*n*	*o*	*p*

Source: Reproduced, with permission, from Market Facts, Inc., *Product Evaluation: An Examination of Research Procedures* (March 1962), p. 30.

Sixteen different soft drink formulas were created expressly for the conduct of the experiment. These consisted of all possible combinations of four different levels of flavor intensity and sugar content. Each product variation (*a, b, c,* etc.) was administered to a different group of respondents. Each respondent rated the degree he liked the variation he drank on a scale ranging from 0 to 10. The performance of each variation was measured in terms of the average preferred score of the respondents exposed to it.

This example is known as a 4^2 factorial. Two variables, each at four levels, are simultaneously evaluated. The results generated by the experiment provide answers to the following four questions:

1. What is the effect of varying flavor intensity on customer preference for the product?
2. What is the effect of varying sugar content on customer preference for the product?
3. To what extent, if any, does the effect of varying flavor intensity on customer preference depend on the level of the product's sugar content?
4. To what extent, if any, does the effect of varying sugar content on customer preference depend on the level of the product's flavor intensity?

When contrasted with the completely randomized designs, the factorial design has a number of advantages. In the soft drink example, suppose it was desirable to have a sample size of 640 individuals. This would amount to exposing 40 individuals to each of the 16 product variations. If we wanted to contrast the performance of each of the four treatments for sugar content, we could compare the average score for all individuals exposed to each of the four treatments regardless of the flavor intensity. This amounts to comparing four averages, each of which is based on a sample of the responses of 160 individuals. A similar procedure would be followed as a basis for comparing the performance of different levels of flavor intensity, except that the averages would be computed with regard to the level of sugar content involved. Once more the comparison would be based on a sample size of 160 for each of the four groups.

Suppose a simple design, say a completed randomized design, had been used to test separately the effects of each of these two

Table **3.9** Sixteen Area Multimedia Experimental Design

	No Newspapers				Newspapers			
	No Radio		Radio		No Radio		Radio	
	No TV	TV	No TV	No TV	No TV	TV	No TV	TV
No outdoor	1	2	3	4	5	6	7	8
Outdoor	9	10	11	12	13	14	15	16

Source: Reproduced, by permission, from G. H. Brown, "Measuring the Sales Effectiveness of Alternative Media," *Seventh Annual Conference of the Advertising Research Foundation* (October 1961).

variables. Suppose, further, that a sample size of 640 was required by the user of the data. Two experiments would be conducted. Each one would have four treatments, with 160 households exposed to each treatment, for a grand total of 1280 households. In other words, by using a factorial design to experiment simultaneously with these two variables, the sample size required was cut in half (1280 to 640). In addition, the factorial design permits estimates to be made as to the answers to questions 3 and 4 which cannot be answered via the use of a completely randomized design.

Because of these inherent characteristics the factorial design has been used in a wide variety of situations. Table 3.9 reports the design of a 2^4 factorial diagram used by the Ford Motor Company [25]. The four variables were newspaper, radio, television, and outdoor billboard coverage. Two levels of each variable were used. One level was zero and the other was a relatively high level of use for each of the media. Each of the 16 combinations of media coverage was exposed to a different geographic area. A measure of actual sales was used as the basis for evaluating the effect of varying expenditures on each of the four media.

A 2^3 factorial design was used to measure the effect on chicken sales (broilers) of varying the nature of the cut packaged and varying the presence and types of recipe included in the package [26]. In another experiment (a 2^4 factorial) effect of varying the type and size of packaging on cheddar cheese sales was investigated [158].

Table 3.10 reports the design of an experiment aimed at meas-

Table **3.10**   Experimental Design Used in Measuring Effect of Advertising on Cookware Sales

| | Fall 1962 | | |
Winter 1963	10 daytime ads per week	5 daytime ads per week	No ads
7 daytime ads per week	Detroit Springfield	Dayton	Wichita
3 daytime ads per week	Columbus	St. Louis Bangor Youngstown	Rochester
No ads	Omaha	Pittsburgh	Philadelphia Grand Rapids

Source: Reproduced, with permission, from J. Becknell, Jr. and Robert W. McIsaac, "Test Marketing Cookware Coated with Teflon," *Journal of Advertising Research,* Vol. 5 (September 1963).

uring the effect of varying the level of advertising and the sequence of levels over time on the sales of cookware [19]. The cities named are those receiving each combination of advertising level and time sequence.

Covariance Analysis. Thus far in our discussion of alternative experimental designs we have concentrated primarily on methods for directly controlling or reducing the heterogeneity of the test units exposed to a given treatment by the experimenter. Randomized blocks, the latin square, and the double change-over designs are examples of the principle of direct control. In each of these designs, one or more variables (such as time period and store) that were apt to generate high levels of heterogeneity from one test to another were directly controlled (held constant at one or more levels) in such a way that their contribution to heterogeneity among test units was partially, if not completely, removed.

It is not always possible to control directly all the variables that are apt to contribute to the heterogeneity of the test units used in an experiment. For example, we cannot control the number of customers who enter a supermarket, nor can we control the prices of competing products. Uncontrolled variation in the magnitude of variables such as these can cause a material loss in the precision of an experiment by increasing the variability of the criterion under investigation (sales of a given product) within the test units being exposed to a given treatment.

Covariance analysis is a statistical procedure which can be used in conjunction with any of the aforementioned experimental designs to increase the precision of the experiment. Its value is only beginning to be recognized in the application of experimental procedure to marketing problems. It can be used to remove the effects of one or more uncontrolled variables on the degree of heterogeneity among test units. In the paragraphs which follow we will provide a graphic illustration of the logic underlying this approach. Our illustration will be confined to taking out the effect of only one variable; however, the logic can be extended to cases involving more than a single "covariate."

Suppose a completely randomized design has been chosen for the study of the effect of varying the level of advertising expenditures for a perishable food product. Suppose, further, that three levels of advertising expenditures are used (T_1, T_2, T_3). Each level of expenditure is exposed to five different cities. In each city ten supermarkets are audited during a two-week period. The per transaction sales of the ten stores are averaged and the resulting figure for each of the 15 cities is the criterion of performance to be used as the basis for determining the effect of the three different levels of advertising expenditure. Suppose at the same time the average price of the product relative to competing products was also measured in each of the 15 cities, and suppose there were no treatment effects. Figure 3.2a presents a hypothetical plot of the per transaction sales (Y) in each of the 15 cities against the product's price relative to competing products (X). This result would be observed if X were related to Y and, further, if varying the level of advertising expenditure had had no effect on sales. It is often convenient to assume that the values plotted cluster around a straight line.

Now suppose, in fact, that three treatments did influence sales. Figure 3.2b pictures such a condition. The average per transaction sales for each of the three treatments is indicated by M_1, M_2, and M_3, respectively. Now suppose we fit three parallel straight lines through each group of five observations (T_1, T_2, T_3). The lines describe the average change in per transaction sales that corresponds to a one-unit change in price within each of the three treat-

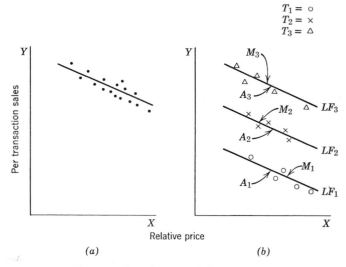

Fig. 3.2   Covariance analysis illustration.

ments. Taking price into account in this fashion has two effects on the results of our experiment. First, one reason accounting for the difference in the three means (M_1, M_2, M_3) is that the three samples of five cities are not comparable in terms of the average relative price for the product under investigation. For example, T_1 has higher relative prices than T_3. This tends to deflate T_1's mean relative to that of T_3. One way to adjust for this fact is to take a given value of X (for example, its mean across all treatments) and use the expected sales per transaction for each treatment (A_1, A_2, A_3) as the basis for making a comparison of the relative effects of the different treatments. This in effect is a device analogous to blocking, except that we attempt to insure the comparability of the treatment through the use of a statistical procedure rather than by specifying in advance that each treatment be administered to the same number of low-, medium-, and high-priced markets.

The use of the linear association between Y and X also has the effect of reducing the amount of variation in Y from one test unit to another within each treatment. The degree of precision associated with the experiment without the use of relative price as a covariate would be measured by the amount of deviation of Y for each test unit from its respective mean (M_1, M_2, or M_3). When price is included as a covariate, the relevant measure of precision is the deviation of each Y from its associated linear function (LF_1, LF_2, LF_3). The magnitude of these deviations is less than those from M_1, M_2, M_3. Thus the precision of the experiment is increased through the use of relative price as a covariate.

This type of analysis can be extended to include more than one covariate at a time. The most important assumption underlying the validity of this approach is that the values of the covariate are in no way influenced by the treatments. For a more detailed discussion of this as well as other assumptions underlying the use of covariance see Cox [45] and Banks [15] as well as Federer [70] and Cochran and Cox [37].

Covariance analysis has been used in conjunction with a latin square design in a study of the effect of various packaging and display conventions on the sale of McIntosh apples [101]. The treatments were blocked on stores and days. The covariate was the number of customers. A customer was defined as one or more persons shopping together and buying a common lot of merchandise. On each of the four days, in each of the four stores, a count of the number of customers was made. The principle involved in using customer count as a covariate was the same as discussed in the preceding illustration. The use of number of customers as a covariate reduced the degree of experimental error by approximately 60 per cent over what it would have been had only a 4 x 4 latin square been used. Those interested in an even more extensive use of covariance analysis should see Henderson, Hind, and Brown [102].

Limitations of experimentation

In the paragraphs which follow we discuss some of the principal limitations associated with the application of experimental techniques to marketing problems.[1]

1. Experiments are often limited to the measurement of short-term response, whereas long-term response is often more relevant to the problem. In addition, the long-term response of a given

[1]The review of limitations is largely paraphrased from an unpublished paper by John Howard and Harry Roberts, entitled "Experimentation in Marketing: An Appraisal."

treatment is often quite different than the short-term response. For example, suppose the advertising expenditures for a certain ethical drug were increased by 50 per cent in an experiment. The effect of such a change on sales may not be evident for quite some time. Many patients may have prescriptions that permit automatic refills. Even if doctors are more apt to prescribe the drug as a result of the advertising, only a small proportion of total demand for the product may consist of new prescriptions. Thus the result of the advertising increase on each would be hardly observable in the short run, whereas in the long run we might find a considerable difference in response.

The longer an experiment is run, the greater the chance that something will happen to "foul" it up. A competitor might introduce a new product or the sales manager responsible for the cities being used as a test unit might refuse to continue a low level of advertising if he observed that sales were declining as a result. No wonder the most extensive work in experimentation thus far has been concerned with direct-mail advertising and with grocery store merchandising of *perishable* food products.

2. The expense of accurately measuring sales in individual test units is often relatively great. When retail stores are the unit, although measurement is easier it nonetheless may involve special store audits. Worse yet is the situation where sales territories are the experimental unit. Often a manufacturer may have shipment but not retail sales data, by territory. One of the most expensive measurement situations occurs when families are the experimental units. Acquiring valid measures of sales may require either repeated interviews or the use of some type of diary. These procedures are not only expensive but they also run the risk of conditioning the respondent by the very process used to measure the response.

3. The variability of sales from one test unit to another is often quite great by comparison with the probable response to the factor being experimentally manipulated. The amount of fluctuation from test unit to test unit regardless of the product involved or the type of test unit (household, city, store, etc.) is often surprisingly large. The greater the degree of this uncontrolled variation, the less valuable will be the results generated from a given experiment.

The existence and magnitude of uncontrolled variation in test-unit sales intensify the need for rigorous analysis of the extent of this variation as part of the procedure involved in the design of an experiment. Only with a careful analysis of this sort can it be determined if the experiment is worth conducting.

4. Often contamination is difficult to prevent. For example, it would be quite difficult to prevent experimental group members in a sales training experiment from talking with members of the control group and/or of other test groups. Similarly, stores often have overlapping trading areas and cities have overlapping television station coverage.

5. It is often difficult to run experiments for long periods of time when they require people in an organization to behave differently than they usually would. In an experiment in which the amount of shelf space devoted to a grocery product was to be manipulated, store managers were quite adept at finding ways to avoid or delay making the necessary changes. In many of the supermarket experiments "enumerators" have been used to check each test unit to be sure that the instructions necessary for the conduct of the experiment were being carried out.

In addition, if people are the test unit, and if they are aware that they are participating in an experiment, they might well change this behavior. For example, sales trainees who are members of an experimental group might improve their productivity because they felt privileged at being included in the experiment and not because of the effect of the particular training procedure. Fortunately, although people are the test units in an experiment, they often need not be told this for the experiment to be conducted.

6. Often an experiment cannot be made sufficiently realistic to be useful. Suppose a product's advertising budget is primarily devoted to national media which have neither regional editions nor provision for split runs. An experiment aimed at evaluating the effect of changing total advertising expenditures would have to make use of media that normally would not be used to promote the product. In addition, competitors will often not respond to tests in the same fashion as they would if the actions taken were part of the company's general policy.

7. More serious security problems are associated with experiments than with other forms of research. A field experiment by

definition reveals the alternatives that management is interested in evaluating. On rare occasions a competitor spots a new product in test market and markets the product himself before the firm doing the testing.

8. The mortality of test units is often relatively high. During the course of an experiment sales territories may change, a salesman might be fired, a store might burn down, a consumer might move, etc.

In spite of these limitations, the application of experimentation to marketing problems will probably continue to grow in scale during the coming years.

Nonexperimental Techniques

A number of multivariate statistical techniques have been developed which when combined with good judgment in the design of an investigation help to provide the type of safeguards that are provided by intervention, control groups, matching, and randomization in experimental studies. The most important of these are discussed in the pages that follow.

1. Regression and correlation analysis
2. Multiple discriminant analysis
3. Factor analysis
4. Canonical analysis
5. Cluster analysis

The potentialities of techniques 4 and 5, in terms of their applications in marketing, are just beginning to be explored, while there are already a number of published studies which employ one or more of the other three procedures.

Correlation and regression

Correlation and regression are techniques for measuring the degree of association between a criterion (dependent) variable and one or more predictors (independent) variables. Regression analysis is appropriate when the magnitude of one variable is to be predicted from knowledge of one or more other variables, whereas correlation analysis is more appropriate where interest centers on the degree of association between a set of measurements. Concepts associated with the two techniques are sufficiently similar to permit their being treated under the same heading. Their logical structure is general enough so as to make them useful as techniques for applying to answer a wide range of questions:

1. What is the relationship between the amount of a given product purchased by a household and its socioeconomic, personality, and/or media exposure characteristics?

2. On the average, will a 10 per cent cut in the price of a given brand have greater impact on its market share than increasing retail advertising by 10 per cent?

3. How useful are measures of general economic activity such as gross national product or per cent unemployed, as predictors of annual sales of refrigerators?

4. To what extent can the sales rate in each of several hundred sales territories for a given ethical drug be predicted on the basis of factors such as disease incidence, number and types of doctors, and/or population and educational distribution?

Although the relevant variables differ from question to question, the nature of the analytical problem (finding some measure of the predictive ability of a set of variables and/or their relative degree of association) is the same. One other characteristic all four have in common is that the criterion variable is continuous (for example, the quantity purchase, refrigerator sales, market share). Regression and correlation techniques are appropriate in cases where the criterion variable is continuous, whereas multiple discriminant analysis (to be discussed in the following section) is appropriate for situations in which the criterion variable is discrete.

Regression and correlation procedures are aimed at achieving the following objectives:

1. Determining the extent to which a set of independent variables are capable of predicting a given dependent variable.

2. Determining the *absolute* as well as the *relative* degree of association between each of a number of independent variables and a dependent variable.

The following actual case histories are presented to illustrate the nature and value of the results generated by regression or cor-

relation analysis. The statistical properties of regression and correlation models are not discussed. Those interested in pursuing the
topic further will find it covered in almost any intermediate level
statistics text, for example, Dixon and Massey [56], Snedecor [160],
and Ezekiel and Fox [66]. For a somewhat more advanced discussion see Anderson and Bancroft [9] or Johnston [109].

Frank and Boyd [73] published a multiple correlation analysis
of the relationship between household private brand consumption
and selected household characteristics, namely, socioeconomic factors, total consumption of the product, and store shopping habits.
In recent years private brands (that is, brands owned by retailers
and distributors as opposed to manufacturers) have been used as
a tool by retailers to differentiate their offerings from those of
manufacturers and competing retailers. One measure of the extent
of their success in achieving this goal is the degree to which private
brands are bought by different types of customers (customers with
different socioeconomic characteristics) than are manufacturers'
brands.

Frank and Boyd conducted separate analyses for 44 grocery
products (for example, regular coffee, frozen orange juice concentrate). The dependent variable in their analysis was the proportion
of purchases for a given product that a household devoted to
private brands. The independent variables were 14 household
socioeconomic characteristics, the total amount of the product
purchased by the household, and five measures of store shopping
behavior.

By using multiple correlation procedures they were able to obtain an estimate of the total degree of association between the
dependent variable (private brand purchasing) and the full set of
20 independent variables. In addition, the analytical procedures
provided an estimate of the *net* degree of association between each
independent variable and private brand purchasing. This is a
measure of the degree of association between one independent
variable and household private brand purchases, while adjusting
for the effect of the other variables included in the analysis (that
is, statistically attempting to hold the effects of the other variables
constant).

The fact that correlation (as well as regression) procedures provide a way of measuring the net association of each of a number of independent variables constitutes one of the principal advantages associated with the use of multivariate procedures.

The Frank and Boyd study found virtually no association between household socioeconomic or total consumption characteristics and private brand purchasing. The only differences observed came as no surprise. Households with members that shop in grocery stores with substantial private branding programs spend a higher percentage of their purchases on private brands.

In another study Frank and Massy [75] were concerned with determining the effect of changing the price, the value of deals (that is, cents off coupons or packs), or the amount of weekly retail advertising for a given brand of a frequently purchased food product, on the brand's weekly market share. Management wanted to improve their estimate of the effect of changing prices, dealing, or advertising on the demand for their product. The analysis started with information about the brand's weekly market share for a two-year period, its weekly price in relation to competing brands, dealing activity relative to competitors, and retail advertising space, relative to competing brands. By the appropriate use of multiple regression procedures they were able to develop estimates of the effect of changes in pricing, dealing, and retail advertising activity on the brand's market share.

A third illustration concerns the use of multiple regression and correlation techniques to help establish expected levels of sales performance in sales territories for a pharmaceutical manufacturer. Sales data were collected for each territory in the firm's organization. In addition, for each territory, data measures were made of general sales determinants such as the number of doctors and the distribution of the population. Regression procedures were used to develop an expected sales figure given "general sales determinants." The difference between expected and actual sales could then be used as a partial criterion for judging the performance of individual salesmen.

The preceding examples illustrate the diverse nature of the marketing problems to which regression and correlation techniques have been applied. They have been used in marketing more often than any of the other multivariate procedures.

Multiple discriminant analysis

Many marketing decisions depend, in part, on management's assumptions as to what factors are associated with (or determine) some aspect of individual or institutional behavior that is defined as a multichotomous as opposed to a continuous variable. For example, in designing the promotional campaign for a particular make of car, it would be desirable to know what characteristics (socioeconomic, personality, etc.) differentiate customers who purchase it from those who purchase, say, each of the three major competing makes in a given price class. The same firm might also benefit from the knowledge of what factors differentiate customers who buy one model from those who buy another. There is similar interest in determining characteristics that discriminate between light and heavy users, loyal and nonloyal customers, customers who shop in one type of outlet as opposed to another, etc. Similarly, the interest may lie in developing a basis for predicting which salesman will achieve above as opposed to below average performance relative to expectations.

Each of these problems has one important common characteristic, namely, the question: What factors are associated with the probability that a given unit (household, salesmen, retail outlet) will fall into one of several categories? That is, they are concerned with the prediction of a multichotomous attribute such as whether a customer buys brand *A, B,* or *C* or whether she shops in store *A* or *B*.

Standard regression and correlation analysis, except when dealing with two groups, cannot be adapted to the prediction of other than continuous variables such as market share or total consumption. Fortunately a technique has been developed for the prediction of multichotomous variables — it is multiple discriminant analysis.

This technique can be used to serve three objectives:

1. Predict an individual's (or institution's) group assignment to one of two or more categories on the basis of his scores on a set of measured characteristics. For example, an automobile insurance company might attempt to develop a model which would predict whether an applicant would be more apt to be accident

prone (that is, have one or more accidents during the next three years) or accident free based on his past driving record and socioeconomic characteristics.

2. Test whether the sample groups have come from a single population versus two or more populations. This test is logically analogous to measuring the degree of multiple correlation. It is a test of the degree to which the independent variables can predict the dependent variable.

3. Determine the relative importance of each predictor variable in making "optimal" assignments of individuals to test categories. Regression analysis provides a measure of both the *absolute* and *relative* importance of a given variable with respect to the degree of its association with the dependent variables. Discriminant analysis provides an estimate *only of the relative* importance of each independent variable.

In 1963 Frank, Massy, and Morrison [76] reported a study of Folger's (a brand of regular coffee) introduction into the Chicago market. The investigators were interested in the answer to the following question: To what extent, if any, can one predict which households would adopt Folger's after its introduction, based on knowledge of household socioeconomic and purchasing characteristics before the introduction? Folger's was introduced in Chicago in early 1959. The researchers had a three-year purchase-by-purchase record of regular coffee consumption from January 1958 through December 1960 for 500 households who belonged to the *Chicago Tribune's* consumer panel during the period. They chose to work with two extreme groups: (a) those households who since late 1959 (well after the introductory period) bought Folgers more often than any other brand; and (b) those households that never bought it at all during the same period (hereafter referred to as *Primary Adopters* and *Nonadopters*). For each household in each of these two groups the researchers took measures of their socioeconomic characteristics and a number of purchase characteristics (for example, the total amount of regular coffee consumed, degree of brand loyalty) during 1958 and early 1959 (before Folger's was introduced into the market). In other words, they had data on two groups of households — primary adopters

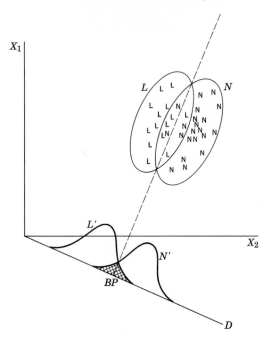

Fig. 3.3   Discriminant illustration.

and nonadopters. For each household in each group they also had measures of 20 socioeconomic and purchase characteristics.

Figure 3.3 presents a graphic illustration of the logic underlying their analysis. Suppose we attempted to predict which group (adopter or nonadopter of Folger's) a household would enter, based on knowledge of two household characteristics before the introduction, say, income (X_1) and total consumption of the product (X_2). Each L in the figure represents the plot of a loyal household in terms of the magnitude of its income and total regular coffee consumption prior to Folger's introduction. Each N represents the plot of a nonloyal household.

Now let us add a third dimension to our figure — height. In effect, the figure consists of two hills: one for adopters and one for nonadopters. Look at any square of the figure. The relative height of the two hills in that square represents a measure of the relative likelihood that a household with any combination of income and consumption, which would place it in that square, will be an adopter or a nonadopter of Folger's. Our problem of prediction becomes one of finding a way of dividing up the two hills so that our "fence" does the best possible job of separating them (provided that the fence itself falls in a straight line). This amounts to plotting a straight line that as nearly as possible coincides with the intersection of the two "hills." This line is drawn as the breakpoint (*BP*). We would predict that any household falling to its left is more apt to be an adopter, whereas any falling to its right would be classified as a nonadopter.

The two curves *L'* and *N'* represent side views to the two hills. The discriminant analysis generates a score for each household. We will call it *D*. Think of the *D* score as placing a household on the *D*-axis of our graph. If the *D* score is greater than the point at which our fence intersects with the *D*-axis, then we would predict that the household would be a nonadopter, whereas if it were less than this value we would predict that it would become a primary adopter.

Discriminant analysis has been used to study a wide variety of problems. Evans [65] used it in a study of the extent to which a household's socioeconomic and personality characteristics would predict which of two brands of cars (Chevrolet or Ford) it purchased. Banks [17] used it to study the difference between brands of food products on the basis of product attributes. King [114] used it to study the use of various market measurements in discriminating between "high" and "low" potential sales territories. Massy [134] has used it to predict FM audience membership based on characteristics such as household and socioeconomic variables, asset ownership, and music preference. Claycamp [34] used it to determine the extent to which thrift deposit owners were systematically different in terms of their socioeconomic and personality characteristics than owners of other types of saving accounts.

For a detailed discussion of the logic underlying discriminant analysis see Massy [135] and Kendall [112].

Factor analysis

The term "factor analysis" represents a group of techniques that are used to analyze the intercorrelations within a set of variables. No particular variable is singled out as a criterion or a "dependent" variable. This group of techniques is used to achieve one or more of four objectives, as described by Massy [136]. These objectives are as follows:

1. Finding a set of dimensions that are latent in a set of variables. Factor analysis was first developed because of a problem faced by psychologists, namely, the measuring of an individual's personality. Suppose we had constructed a personality test in which an individual had to answer 100 multiple-choice questions. Do these questions really measure 100 different aspects of his personality? How can we find a smaller set of variables that somehow summarize the information contained in the original set of 100 scores for each individual? The techniques included under the label of factor analysis are devices for looking at the problem of intercorrelations between the original 100 scores and deducing from this which subset of scores are highly intercorrelated and hence seem to be measuring somewhat the same dimensions.

2. Finding a way to group people into distinctly different groups which exist in a larger population. The question of the extent and nature of market segmentation is focused on questions such as: To what extent do segments of households exist whose purchasing habits are distinctly different from those of another segment? Given a set of measured "purchasing habits" (for example, proportion of purchases devoted to brands A, B, C, etc.) we could use factor analytic techniques to determine the extent and nature of household segmentation (for example, in terms of the similarity of the mix of brands they purchase).

3. Identifying likely variables for subsequent regression analysis. Frank and Boyd [74] used factor analytic techniques as an aid in determining which household socioeconomic variables to delete from a regression analysis in which they were trying to predict household private brand consumption for grocery products based on socioeconomic characteristics. Factor analysis provided a measure of the extent to which the various socioeconomic characteristics were intercorrelated.

The potential independent variables which are highly correlated can be looked upon as containing a great deal of redundant information. There is no reason for including both of them in an analysis. For example, age of husband and housewife is quite highly correlated. Whatever degree the age of housewife is apt to be associated with private brand consumption, so will age of husband. One of the variables should be excluded from the analysis. It is impossible in this situation to make statements about the effect of husband's age or wife's age on private brand consumption. All we can do is determine what difference there is between younger and older households with respect to private brand consumption.

4. Creating an entirely new set of variables for inclusion in regression, discriminant or cluster analysis. This application is similar to that discussed in objective 3 except that new variables are created and used in subsequent analysis, which are weighted averages of the original variables. The weights are generated by the factor analysis. Original variables having a high weight in the calculation of a particular new variable (a factor score) represent one subset of variables that have relatively high intercorrelations with each other.

In addition to the aforementioned examples, factor analytic techniques have been applied in a number of different situations. Twedt reports a study of the determinants of advertising readership [174]. For each of the 137 ads, 20 measures of advertising content (for example, number of words in an ad, number of product characteristics mentioned) and mechanical characteristics (size of ad, headline size, color) were factor analyzed. The result of this factor analysis revealed that the 20 original variables were highly intercorrelated. Of the 20, only seven really represented different dimensions of an ad's description. These seven variables were then used in subsequent regression analyses to determine their association with ad readership.

Farley reports a study of the characteristics associated with variation in the level of brand loyalty from one food product category to another [67]. He used factor analysis to achieve the same objectives as Twedt, but he went one step further; he used the technique to generate a "new" set of summary variables and then used the "new" variables as predictors in a regression analysis.

Harper factor analyzed the results of 13 quality tests for cheddar cheese [97]. Three critical dimensions of cheese quality were identified and used as the basis for a quality control program.

In none of the examples we have presented is factor analysis viewed as a technique that competes with regression, correlation, or discriminant analysis. Factor analysis is most appropriately viewed as complementary and not a competing procedure. It is seldom that the same problem requires the use of both multiple regression and discriminant analysis. Quite often, however, factor analysis can be used to advantage in conjunction with one of the other multivariate statistical techniques.

Canonical correlation

A useful device to help understand the purpose of canonical correlation is to contrast it with ordinary multiple correlation, which we have previously discussed. Multiple correlation procedures were concerned with finding the degree of linear association between a *single* dependent variable and *more than one* independent variables. Canonical correlation procedures are designed to measure simultaneously the interrelationships between *more than one* (a set of) dependent variables and *a set* of independent variables, each consisting of measurements on the same individuals or institutions.

The potentialities of applying canonical correlation procedures in marketing are unexplored. Only one article on the subject [86] has appeared in the marketing literature. In our opinion, however, this situation will gradually change. There are a number of problems whose logical structure came close to that for which canonical correlation is designed. For example, suppose one is interested in predicting salesmen's performance based on such factors as individual socioeconomic characteristics, personality traits, and past employment. The concept of "performance" is a complex one. Usually we are interested in a number of criteria such as number of calls per week, number of new accounts, and number of special displays. Restated in terms of the logic of canonical correlation, we have a set of dependent variables for each salesman (number of calls, number of new accounts, etc.) and a set of independent variables (socioeconomic characteristics, personality traits, etc.). Interest focuses on the extent of correlation between the *set* of dependent and the *set* of independent variables.

This same type of analogy can also be made for certain studies of customer buying behavior. For each of a number of customers there may be a set of measures of purchasing behavior (total consumption, brand loyalty) for a product, together with a *set* of possible predictors such as personality and socioeconomic characteristics. Stated in this fashion, the problem closely resembles the structure of our preceding example.

For a discussion of the statistical theory underlying canonical correlation procedures (beyond that presented by [86]) the reader should see Anderson [10], Kendall [113], or Cooley and Lohnes [43].

Cluster analysis

The term cluster analysis refers to the various analytical procedures which have been designed for the purpose of simultaneously assessing the similarity between observations such as individuals or cities, based on "profiles" of their scores on a number of measured characteristics. This objective (establishing similar groups of observations) is quite different from that of either regression, correlation, discriminant, or canonical analysis. In each of these procedures the order of the observations in terms of group membership is done in advance via its measured score on whatever variable is chosen as the dependent variable. In cluster analysis no advance assignment of observations to groups is made in advance. Instead, one of the principal objectives of the analysis is to find what clusters (groups) of observations are "similar" with respect to their "profile." In addition, these techniques are useful for determining some "best" number of clusters (or groups) into which a given population may be divided.

To date cluster analysis is virtually an unknown technique in marketing research. In spite of this fact, it is designed to provide an analytical basis for testing a critical class of assumptions that underlie some of the most important policy decisions that are made in marketing. For example, suppose we are considering introducing a new brand into the market for an established product. Which of the existing brands will the new brand (object) be most similar to? Given data describing the various characteristics of each brand, cluster techniques could be used as a partial basis for identifying brands with similar profiles.

One concept gaining widespread popularity in marketing is

"market segmentation." The crucial trick underlying the profitable segmentation of markets is for management to be able to determine a way of grouping customers in terms of the nature of their demand for the product in question so that customers within a given group (that is, market segment) are quite similar in terms of the profile of their demand characteristics. Presumably if one market has been successfully segmented, a way has been found to divide it so that the customers belonging to each segment are relatively similar in contrast to the differences that exist from group to group. Given a set of measured characteristics for a number of customers, cluster analysis can potentially be used as a device for empirically determining the number and composition of such market segments.

An example of still a different application of cluster analysis is provided by work which the authors are just completing [85]. The problem of selecting test markets has long plagued researchers. It would be desirable to choose a test market or test markets which are similar as possible to other market areas so that if the product is introduced nationally the test market results will be reasonably accurate indicators of national performance. The number and choice of test markets used in a study depends in part on how many different groups of markets the researcher believes there are, and along what dimension or dimensions the markets are to be grouped. That is, given a number of objects (market areas) and each of their "profiles" with respect to a number of measured characteristics such as per capita income, population, per cent college trained, the researcher might ask: (a) How many similar groups of markets are there? and (b) Which markets fall into which groups?

The intriguing potentialities of cluster analysis are just beginning to be explored in marketing. Readers interested in a more detailed discussion should see Cronbach and Gleser [51] and Rao [144].

Multivariate Techniques and Marketing; Some Concluding Comments

In our opinion the application of both experimental and nonexperimental multivariate statistical techniques will continue to increase in marketing as increased familiarity with these procedures is gained by personnel working in the field. In recent years packaged computer programs have been developed and are now available for use in a large number of computer installations throughout the country. These programs are designed to handle the computational requirements of every analytical technique we have considered in this chapter as well as many more. The computation problem has been reduced from one requiring the services of a large number of clerks a fair amount of time to one necessitating filling out a few control cards (which tell the computer how your data is organized and what you want done with it). The time-consuming part of the research process becomes the design and interpretation phases and not the computational steps.

Virtual elimination of the computational problem is especially important in the context of marketing. Given our lack of knowledge of the factors that affect market and/or customer behavior, it is frequently necessary to conduct exploratory studies based on large masses (large in terms of both number of observations and number of variables) of data. Multivariate techniques provide us with a much more powerful set of tools for effectively extracting information from large data bases. Man has a hard enough time thinking about the relationships between more than two or three variables at once, let alone considering 15, 20, or 50. By using the computer's computational capabilities, together with the logical procedures embodied in the techniques discussed in this chapter, management has a start on the technological basis for substantially extending its analytical powers when dealing with the formulation and analysis of marketing programs.

4 Mathematical Modeling of Marketing Processes

Introduction

To an increasing extent marketing researchers are utilizing techniques and approaches drawn from the disciplines of the management sciences — operations research, systems engineering, econometrics, and the computer sciences. In Chapters 2 and 3 we stressed the measurement aspects of marketing research. This has been by design and based on our feeling that a primary reason for the limited application of mathematical models to marketing is due to a dearth of relevant measurements of marketing effects and our comparative lack of understanding of marketing phenomena.

In this chapter we attempt to describe recent innovations in the modeling of marketing processes and the techniques which have been developed for "solving" perennial problems:

1. How much should we spend on marketing effort and how should it be allocated over products, territories, media, consumer versus trade channels, etc.?
2. How many items should be in our product line and how should they be priced?
3. How should new product candidates be evaluated and what is the appropriate timing for new product introduction?
4. How many distribution points — warehouses, retail outlets — should we have and where should they be located?

The questions that we could list are almost limitless. Unfortunately, our experience in answering these complex questions is definitely limited, if not actually meager.

108

In this chapter we discuss the progress to date in the design and application of mathematical models. We first describe briefly the general nature of the model-building process and its evolution in marketing. We next discuss specific problem classes — allocation, inventory, competitive, queuing problems — and describe typical marketing illustrations which display the characteristics of these problem classes.

In the next section of the chapter we discuss various techniques for solving models, including so-called "optimization" methods (for example, the marginal analysis of economic theory, mathematical programming) and simulation.

Our attention then turns to specific applications of mathematical modeling in marketing and the nature of current research in model building. Finally, we appraise the status of management science in marketing research and describe some of the limitations of these models.

The Nature and Evolution of Model Building in Marketing

We have already encountered several "models" in earlier chapters — the Bayesian model in Chapter 1, various behavioral models in Chapter 2 and a variety of statistical models in Chapter 3. As we have seen, a model consists of a *representation of some real system, expressed basically in terms of a series of "if . . . then" statements and containing some specifications on how variables in the model should be measured.*

Management scientists, for the most part, have been concerned with *prescriptive* models of the type: "given a desire to maximize something — profits, cash flow — subject to some constraints, that is, some type of resource limitations, one should choose a course of action which is 'best' (in the sense just described)." Most management science models, then, are used for making policy recommendations. This is not to say, of course, that the model does not have a descriptive component. Essentially, the model's output is a prediction that the course of action selected will indeed lead to the "best" outcome.

In applying models to marketing problems, the descriptive part of the model presents the major source of difficulty, largely through our lack of understanding of marketing processes. As Simon and Newell [155] have pointed out:

Operations research has made large contributions to those management decisions that can be reduced to systematic computational routines. To date, comparable progress has not been made in applying scientific techniques to judgmental decisions that cannot be so reduced.

In view of this remark, it is not surprising that marketing has been one of the *last* of the functional areas to yield to the modeling techniques of the management scientist.

First, just the specification of the many interrelated courses of action typically associated with marketing problems can be a major task. If a management scientist attempts to develop an "optimal" advertising allocation over products, territories, media, vehicles within medium, frequency of ad insertion, or size of ad, the possibilities can easily run into billions.

Second, management science models typically assume that marketing objectives can all be combined into some common unit of measurement or at least stated as a single measure to be maximized, subject to a set of constraints. As discussed in detail in Chapter 5, we still know very little about value theory and methods for establishing "trade-offs" among conflicting objectives.

Third, control over outcomes is much more difficult to achieve than in counterpart problems arising in production processes. Competitors' actions, distributors' actions and consumers' behavior are extremely difficult to predict, let alone control. The instability of marketing processes is a major problem in designing effective models and measurement techniques.

Finally, testing the validity of models is subject to many difficulties. Typically, there is little opportunity for experimentation in the classical sense of that word. Usually the marketing manager must settle for a careful review of the model's assumption structure, including the interrelationships among the model's components. In some cases limited experiments or retrospective test simulations may be conducted; still the testing and control of model solutions represents a major problem in marketing.

Perhaps these reservations miss the essential point. Although the modeling of marketing processes is hardly a simple task, the fact remains that *any decision presupposes some description, or model of the environment, no matter how vague or judgmental.* If the value of *explicit* model formulation lies more in the kinds of questions to which this activity gives rise (and the kinds of data which need to be specified), the current status of model building appears much less bleak.

Evolution of model building in marketing

Management science — at least as represented by such societies as The Institute of Management Sciences and the Operations Research Society of America — is largely a post-World War II phenomenon. Despite the "youth" of this discipline, management science groups currently exist in virtually every industry and government agency. In the fifties, however, most of the efforts of management scientists were confined to problems in inventory control, production scheduling, equipment replacement and machine maintenance. Among the ten thousand articles, books, and technical papers appearing in this field during the fifties, less than 3 per cent involved marketing problems [83].

During the last ten years, however, interest in marketing problems by management scientists has increased sharply. This trend reflects the progress which had already been made in production problems, the large stakes associated with marketing decisions, and the development of newer techniques for coping with the probabilistic, time-dependent environment of the marketer. We shall describe some of these recent applications after first discussing some specific problem classes for which models have been designed and the techniques that have been developed for solving them.

Problem Classes and Management Science Models

There are many ways of classifying problems, models, and solution techniques. We could start with the basic functional areas of marketing — pricing, product, promotion, distribution, and location decisions — and discuss management science models under these headings; we could describe various solution techniques — linear programming, dynamic programming, and simulation — and comment on problems to which these techniques have been applied; or we could discuss management science models in various marketing situations — industrial marketing, wholesaling, and retailing.

We have elected to discuss models first in terms of *problem* structure, rather than in terms of solution technique. Specific marketing applications will be described after we have discussed the more formal characteristics of the models.

Basic problem types

As Ackoff and Rivett [5] indicate, the management scientist tends to view problems in terms of *structure* rather than content. They list eight basic forms: (a) inventory; (b) allocation; (c) queuing; (d) sequencing; (e) routing; (f) replacement; (g) competition; and (h) search, which singly or in combination have accounted for a large number of problems in general managerial decision making. We shall comment on those problem forms that appear most useful in marketing problem solving. (We follow the Ackoff-Rivett description closely.)

Inventory Problems. As Ackoff and Rivett note, *inventory* consists of idle resources — men, material, machines, money — which can be employed in some activity. The two types of costs associated with idle resources are:

1. Costs that increase as inventory increases, for example, inventory storage, obsolescence, deterioration, insurance, taxes.
2. Costs that decrease as inventory increases, for example, setup and takedown costs, shortage costs, purchase price and direct production costs, production rate costs.

Despite the obvious correspondence of the foregoing descriptions to inventory models, in the narrow sense, many marketing problems display the same structure, although their content may not at first suggest the form of an "inventory" problem. For example, a firm may be interested in the best number of salesmen to keep in training. Too few salesmen-in-training could lead to unmanned sales territories if several incumbent salesmen were terminated for some reason. If too many salesmen-in-training are maintained, the firm incurs standby costs for potential income producers who have not yet been assigned a territory.

The selection of the best time interval for evaluating new products may also be viewed in terms of this model. Too short a time interval for evaluation incurs costs associated with the higher risk of commercializing (or failure to commercialize) a poor (good) product. Too slow an evaluation implies that the firm would defer revenues to a future period and perhaps increase the chances of competitors' imitating or superseding the product.

Other marketing problems that could be cast into the inventory model format include the number of advertisements to pretest, the number and size of retail outlets and supermarket parking facilities to maintain, and the determination of manning levels for technical service personnel. In addition, decisions regarding wholesale and retail stock maintenance and spare parts inventory levels at service depots represent rather straightforward applications of inventory models.

Allocation Problems. An *allocation* problem can be defined as consisting of the following:

1. A set of jobs to be done.
2. A set of alternative means for doing at least some of the jobs, all means not being equally efficient.
3. A lack of resources available to do each job in the best way.

The problem, of course, is to allocate the resources to the jobs so as to maximize some *total* measure of effectiveness. In the case in which each job requires one and only one resource (for example, assigning salesmen to territories), the problem is to find the specific assignment of men to territories that maximizes some figure of merit.

Some jobs may require multiple resources and some resources may be used for more than a single job. If so, the problem is still one of allocation but different solution techniques are involved. Many distribution problems are of this form inasmuch as many firms have multiple supply points and multiple destinations. The problem is to determine how much product to ship from each supply point to each destination.

Product-mix problems are often characterized by the case where potential jobs exceed available means for performing the jobs. How should a salesman allocate his limited time among various classes of accounts? How should a fixed budget for print media be allocated among magazines? How should a limited pool of money be distributed in the form of bonuses among salesmen? How should the marketing researcher allocate his time among projects competing for his attention? Illustrations of this type of allocation problem abound in the marketing field.

In many cases the allocation problem is further complicated by two considerations. First, the manager may wish to solve *simultaneously* for the best total sales budget and its allocation over competing activities. Second, the "return" to activity *A* may be *interrelated* with the level of effort spent on activity *B*. Most realistic marketing problems exhibit both of these complexities. For example, a new product manager may be able to exercise some discretion in determining both the total promotional amount to be spent in the first year of product introduction and how it should be allocated among promotional activities. Second, the effectiveness of spending a specified amount of money on, for example, consumer promotion will depend on the means employed to induce distributors to make the product available.

Frequently the management scientist settles for some subset of the larger allocation problem, assuming that the interaction is sufficiently weak to enable him to "decouple" the subproblem from the larger problem. This tendency to decouple interrelated decisions — to make the problem tractable — is also found in the tendency to treat sequentially dependent decisions as a series of "one-shot" independent decisions. Recent progress in the development of sequential and interactive models, however, should reduce the need for such simplification.

Competitive Problems. Most strategic level marketing problems display some characteristics of this problem form. Essentially, in this class of problems the effectiveness of the decision maker's action is affected by the actions — cooperative or competitive — of other decision makers. A specific decision maker may have varying amounts of information about other decision makers' actions, ranging from almost certain information to virtually no information at all.

In Chapter 1 we discussed the Bayesian model as a framework for dealing with interactive decisions under conditions of partial information. The theory of games has been applied to a very limited extent on this general type of problem as well; most applications have involved military problems.

Competitive bidding for contracts, product pricing, manufacturer-distributor liaisons, cooperative advertising campaigns, establishment of product guarantees, executive recruitment, negotiations for retail display space, and general marketing strategy formulation all take place within a complex environment of competitors, consumers, or regulatory agencies. Although the current theoretical apparatus underlying the analysis of competitive problems is still inadequate for dealing with realistic situations, there is reason to believe that methodological innovations will continue. Certainly the stakes are large and would warrant concerted research in this area of interest.

Other Problem Types. We have limited our detailed discussion to the preceding three classes of problems, inasmuch as most marketing applications to date appear to have fallen principally into one or more of these categories. Although a more complete account can be found in Ackoff and Rivett, some (brief) attention should be given to the other five problem classes which comprise their classification.

Queuing problems are typified by the existence of a facility for serving customers and a probabilistic customer arrival pattern. If the service rate is "too high" relative to customer requirements, idle service time results. If the customer requirements are "too high" relative to service rates, the customers wait in queue, leading to costs associated with waiting. The "customers" may or may not be human beings. The major problem is to design the service facility such that the sum of these two groups of costs is minimized. Obvious examples in marketing concern such services as supermarket check-out booths, the number of operators to maintain in a gasoline service station, the number of clerks to maintain in a retail outlet, and so on. As might be surmised, this class of problems exhibits many similarities with inventory problems.

Sequencing problems are characterized, as the name suggests, by finding a serial order of items which minimizes some cost associated with their processing. So-called critical path techniques are illustrative of this class of solutions. Marketing illustrations would include the scheduling of new product introductions and advertising campaigns.

Routing problems can be illustrated by the classical "traveling salesman" problem in which a salesman has a known number of cities to visit. The problem is to select a route from home city to each city and back home again so as to minimize some measure, for example, distance, time, or travel cost. Examples of this problem class might include model change-over policies and supermarket flow patterns.

Replacement problems can be further subdivided into those involving items whose efficiency decreases with use (or time) and those which fail without previous deterioration, such as light bulbs and vacuum tubes. In the former subclass the problem is usually to determine the time for replacing the item that minimizes the sum of operating (including maintenance) costs and investment outlays. In marketing, the problem of determining advertising campaign length and product life cycle length might be viewed in this context. For nondeteriorating items the problem usually concerns the nature of group replacement plans. Various product-service policies involving equipment maintenance after-the-sale could be analyzed in terms of this format.

Search problems, the last of the Ackoff-Rivett categories, are typified by the need, given a fixed amount of resources, to balance "extensive" versus "intensive" investigation of the characteristics of some process. In marketing research surveys, for example, taking a larger sample usually leads to lower sampling error. If time is limited, however, a larger sample may be associated with a more cursory examination of sampled items, leading to a greater chance for making observational errors. The problem is to design a plan that minimizes some overall function of these risks. Statistical sampling, information retrieval, and store location are but a few of the areas which may be viewed within this context. (The reader should also note its conceptual relationship to Bayesian decision theory, already discussed in Chapter 1.)

The foregoing problem classes are not mutually exclusive and collectively exhaustive and, furthermore, it would be rare if problems — marketing or otherwise — fell neatly into a single problem class. Like most taxonomies, this classification is meant to be suggestive and to illustrate that many seemingly diverse situations can nevertheless exhibit similar structure, although their content may be highly variable. Indeed, the management scientist's preoccupation with "structure" provides a useful and often unique point of view — a natural complement to the manager who is usually concerned with the specific content of problems.

Solution techniques and illustrative models

No attempt is made in this chapter to describe in detail the various techniques which have been proposed for solving marketing models. Rather, our purpose is to illustrate briefly some of the principal solution methods and to point out the underlying assumptions involved in the models for which solutions are sought.

Mathematical models can be broadly delineated into four categories:

1. Deterministic — static
2. Deterministic — time dependent
3. Probabilistic — static
4. Probabilistic — time dependent

In deterministic models the variables in the model are assumed to be "known," whereas in probabilistic models the analyst works with probability distributions of the variables. In static models the solution is "dimensionless" with respect to time; as the name suggests, time-dependent models are concerned with predicting a system's behavior over specified time intervals.

Solutions to models may be obtained by *analytical* or *numerical* means. As Ackoff indicates [2], in obtaining analytical solutions we proceed deductively to the solution. In numerical methods (including simulation) we proceed inductively by trying out various values of the controllable variables and finding out which set yields the best results. Numerical procedures which converge toward a definite solution on successive trials are called iterative; many of the mathematical programming techniques are of this type.

We now proceed to illustrate some of the models and/or solution techniques that have been used in marketing analysis. (We shall later refer to these techniques in our discussion of applications.)

The Calculus. It is not unusual that many of the early applications of models to marketing problems — involving total promotional budget determination and its allocation — used the calculus. These models were essentially deterministic-static, and the calculus provided a convenient means for solving for maxima and minima under either an unconstrained or constrained (for example, some limit on total budget) basis.

As an illustration of the application of the calculus to total promotional budget determination, assume that a firm's unit sales response to promotion [8] can be represented by the equation,

$$Q = a + \sqrt{bX}$$

where Q = sales units per time period, X = dollars of promotion, and a and b are parameters. If we let $a = 500$ and $b = 100$, we obtain the relationship shown in Fig. 4.1.

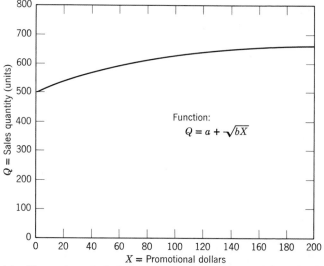

Fig. 4.1   Illustration of diminishing returns on additional promotional expenditures. Reproduced, with permission, from W. Alderson and P. E. Green, *Planning and Problem Solving in Marketing,* (Homewood, Ill.: Richard D. Irwin, 1964), p. 274.

Suppose the firm's net profit is given by the following equation:

$$\pi = PQ - [VQ + F + X]$$

where π = profit, P = price in dollars per unit, V = variable cost per unit, and F = fixed cost. If we let P = \$5.00, V = \$3.00 and F = \$1000, we obtain the curves for total revenue (PQ), total cost ($VQ + F + X$), and profit π, shown in Fig. 4.2.

By using standard techniques of the calculus (setting the derivative of the profit equation with respect to X, the control variable equal to zero, etc.) we obtain the solution $X = \$100$, which maximizes total profit. If we had some constraint on the amount of promotional funds available, we could still solve for the optimal level by using Lagrange techniques [8].

The foregoing model is an illustration of a deterministic-static model. In using the calculus we have assumed that *all* relevant variables are known exactly and that the functions that linked the variables together were "well-behaved" and differentiable. We also

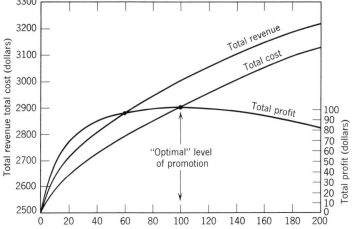

Fig. 4.2   Behavior of total revenue, cost, and profit as a function of promotional expenditures. Reproduced, with permission, from W. Alderson and P. E. Green, *Planning and Problem Solving in Marketing*, (Homewood, Ill.: Richard D. Irwin, 1964), p. 274.

assumed that the solution did not lie on the "boundary" of the profit function. (For linear functions, where extreme values *are* located on the boundary, calculus is of no help.) Although the calculus is mathematically elegant, it is clear from the preceding illustration that the form and values of the variables in the appropriate equations are subject to rather stringent assumptions.

Linear Programming. Many of the relationships with which the analyst works may be approximated by linear (straight line) functions. Linear programming represents a set of procedures for optimizing some linear function subject to a set of linear constraints (as noted earlier, the calculus is of no help here).

To illustrate the use of linear programming in very simple form, assume that a firm is faced with a media allocation problem (Robinson and Luck [149]) involving how many advertising pages to purchase in each of two magazines, 1 and 2. The advertising manager has a monthly budget of $5000 to spend and he wants to maximize the "reach," that is, the number of potential customers who would see a specific one-page ad in the magazine. We also assume that reach is proportional to number of ad pages placed. The reach of magazine 1 is 8000 potential customers and that of magazine 2 is 5000 potential customers per one-page ad. The number of potential customers, however, having incomes under $10,000 per year is 1000 persons and 400 persons per one-page ad seen in magazines 1 and 2, respectively. Furthermore, cost per full-page advertising is $500 and $1000 in 1 and 2, respectively. Suppose, further, that the manager would like to achieve a reach of at most 4000 potential customers whose incomes are less than $10,000 annually. We can summarize this verbalization by:

$$\text{Objective: Maximize } V = 8000\,x_1 + 5000\,x_2$$
$$\text{Subject to} \qquad x_1,\ x_2 \geq 0$$
$$\$\ 500x_1 + \$1000x_2 \leq \$5000$$
$$1000x_1 + \quad 400x_2 \leq \quad 4000$$

Figure 4.3 shows graphically how the solution can be obtained for this oversimplified case. First, the two constraint equations are plotted, leading to the heavy line area of the figure. Next, where the V-function touches the bounded (feasibility) region is determined. The solution is allocate 2.50 pages to magazine 1 and allocate 3.75 pages to magazine 2. If so, 38,750 potential customers will be reached and all constraints will have been satisfied.

In the foregoing formulation we assumed again that all values were known and fixed. (We also made a number of assumptions regarding such terms as "potential customers," "reach," and so on.) Current variations permit varying the values of the variables (parametric programming), using probability distributions of the variables (stochastic programming), or, in some special cases, using nonlinear functions (nonlinear programming). Notice that in our formulation, however, we dealt with the deterministic-static case. Many solution techniques for problems in this model class are available, including the transportation model and the Simplex routine [Kotler 117].

3. *Dynamic Programming.* Oftentimes the analyst must work with interdependent stages where today's decision must be examined in terms of its implications for future time periods, that is, concern is with time-dependent applications. Dynamic programming [20], a technique developed for handling this type of problem, can be used for both the deterministic and probabilistic cases.

In terms of assumptions, dynamic programming is one of the least restrictive allocation models. Functions need not be linear or differentiable. We do not illustrate the technique here, but we should mention that the procedure involves a step-by-step solution process (a recurrence relation) whereby the problem is solved a stage at a time — usually working backwards from some desired end state. This is not unlike our solution of the "box" problem

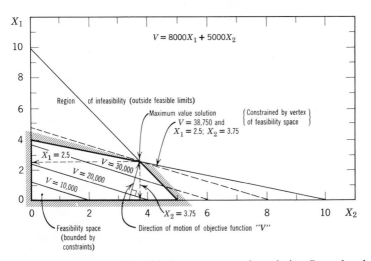

Fig. 4.3 Two-dimensional graphic linear programming solution. Reproduced, with permission, from P. J. Robinson and D. Luck, *Promotional Decision Making: Practice and Theory,* (New York: McGraw-Hill Book Co., 1964), p. 221.

of Chapter 1 which was used to illustrate the application of Bayesian decision theory.

Critical Path Methods. Critical path techniques can be useful for answering the following questions [Kotler 118] regarding the scheduling of a complex activity like the introduction of a new product:

1. What is the best way to sequence various interconnected activities?
2. Given "normal" resources, how long will it take to make the product ready for sale?
3. What extra resources would be required to complete the project some specified number of time periods earlier?

As a simple illustration of one procedure which has been developed (PERT, or Program Evaluation and Review Technique), Kotler lists the following activities (note Fig. 4.4):

    1. Corporate approval granted
    2. Engineering and styling completed
    3. Marketing analysis completed
    4. Advertising campaign plans completed
    5. Manufacturing preparation completed
    6. Market testing completed

After these events are identified, a PERT analysis consists of three steps as follows:

1. *Preparing a program network.* In what order should these events

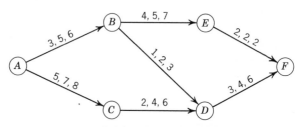

Fig. 4.4 Simplified illustration of PERT network. Reproduced, with permission, from P. Kotler, "The Uses of Mathematical Models in Marketing," *Journal of Marketing,* **27** (October 1963), pp. 36–41.

take place? Certain events will be in a *priority* relationship and others in a *concurrent* relationship.

The best way to see this distinction is to work backward from the terminal event. Before a market test can be started, let alone completed, two prior events must take place. The advertising campaign plans must be completed and the product must be manufactured.

But these two prior events are themselves in a concurrent relationship — the activities leading to the completion of each can be carried on concurrently. The next step would be to examine each of these events separately, to determine what events must precede each. When there are hundreds of events, the task of preparing a "network" for these events is neither easy nor free from ambiguity. But for the six events listed earlier, the most efficient network is fairly straightforward. By representing the events as circles, we would prepare the network shown in Fig. 4.4.

2. *Estimating activity times.* The department responsible for each activity is asked to estimate the *most likely time* to complete that activity, given the department's normal resources. This estimate is supplemented by both an optimistic and pessimistic estimate, again assuming normal department resources. For convenience, the three estimates are connected by commas and placed alongside the activity arrows (Fig. 4.4). As an example, the department responsible for event *B* estimates that it will take between 3 and 6 weeks, with the most likely time being 5 weeks.

3. *Finding the critical path.* What is the earliest time the market test could be completed? It is necessary to trace back through all the paths that must be traveled, and the total time each will take.

There are three paths leading to the market test: *ABEF*, *ABDF*, and *ACDF*. On a *most likely time basis* (a different measure is used in practice), path *ABEF* will take $5 + 5 + 2 = 12$ weeks, path *ABDF* will take $5 + 2 + 4 = 11$ weeks, and path *ACDF* will take $7 + 4 + 4 = 15$ weeks. This last path is therefore considered the *critical path;* since it must be traversed and it consumes the greatest sum of time, it sets the earliest most likely time for completion.

What is equally interesting is that events along a noncritical path such as *ABEF* can take place later than estimated without necessarily delaying the 15-week estimate for the project as a whole. In other words, activities along noncritical paths have some "slack" in their required completion time. In actual applications, the network will be extremely complicated and its characteristics would be very time-consuming to discern through manual calculations. A computer can be used, however, to estimate the likely completion date and the slack times associated with the noncritical activities. Every few weeks a new computation is made, to reflect new information affecting the completion date. Alternative decisions about shifting resources can be simulated to see what effect they would have on completion time.

As Kotler suggests, PERT provides a structured way to plan such marketing activities as new product introductions and advertising campaigns by showing how resources can be reallocated for shortening scheduled times, as well as in assigning responsibility for the completion of certain subtasks. It is a combination of a forecasting and scheduling technique and can be adapted to deal with cases where uncertainty regarding activities or event times must be considered.

Markov Brand-Switching Models. The Markov process model has recently received quite a bit of attention by marketing analysts as a description of consumer brand switching behavior. This model is a good illustration of a probabilistic time-dependent model. As we show later, however, the rather stringent assumptions underlying the model render it, at best, a rather gross description of actual brand-switching behavior. To illustrate the technique we describe a case taken from Green and Tull [91].

In brief, Markov processes deal with a sequence of events over time which, we assume, are generated by a probabilistic process. The Markovian property of the process is that the probability of an event (e.g., customer purchases brand A in time period t) is dependent only on the immediately preceding outcome (for example, customer's last purchase was brand B) and not on events prior to that. For example, suppose we assume that a customer must be in one of three states on her last buying occasion: purchased brand A; purchased brand B; purchased brand C (where C represents "all other" brands). Assume further that by using consumer panel data where each panel participant keeps a diary of purchases over some extended period of time, the marketing researcher is able to estimate transition probabilities. By "transition probabilities" are meant the conditional probabilities of switching from state to state, given the outcome of the previous trial. In a "first-order" Markov process these conditional probabilities refer to the probability of purchasing brand j on the next purchase occasion, given that brand i was

Table **4.1**   Transition Probabilities—Three State Illustration

Last Purchase	Next Purchase			
	A	B	C	Total
A	0.7	0.2	0.1	1.00
B	0.3	0.5	0.2	1.00
C	0.1	0.1	0.8	1.00

purchased on the last buying occasion. Higher-order Markov processes would be required if the probability of purchasing brand j depended on 2, 3, 4, . . ., etc. previous purchases. Table 4.1 presents a set of hypothetical transitional probabilities for the preceding illustration.

As can be noted from Table 4.1, given that a customer purchased brand A on her last buying occasion, the estimated probability of buying brand A on her next buying occasion is 0.7. With probability 0.2 she will switch to brand B and with probability 0.1 she will switch to brand C (all other brands). Similar remarks pertain to the other rows of the transition probability matrix. Notice that since we have defined a set of mutually exclusive, collectively exhaustive states, all row probabilities sum to unity.

To describe the mechanics of a Markov process, suppose a customer starts out in state A, that is, as a buyer of brand A. What is the probability that she will be in states A, B, and C, respectively, on the third buying occasion? To answer this question we could use the methods of matrix algebra. For purposes of simplicity of discussion, however, we can trace out the behavior of this process by using a tree diagram as shown in Fig. 4.5. If we performed the indicated multiplication we would find that after the first, second, and third transitions the probabilities of our brand A purchaser (at the start of the process) being a purchaser of brands A, B, and C are as follows:

	A	B	C
First transition	0.7	0.2	0.1
Second transition	0.56	0.25	0.19
Third transition	0.486	0.256	0.258

We could continue the process indefinitely into the future. If we did, we would find that the probabilities would approach "equilibrium" values; that is, as the number of transitions approached infinity the

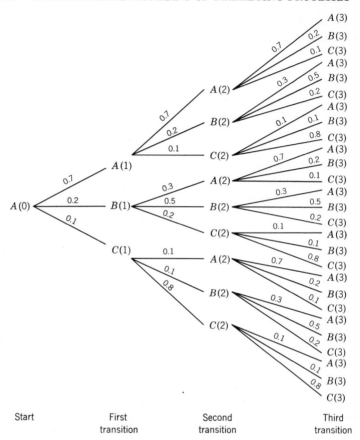

Fig. 4.5   Tree Diagram—Three State Markov process. Reproduced, with permission, from P. E. Green and D. S. Tull, *Research for Marketing Decisions* (Englewood Cliffs, N. J.: Prentice-Hall, 1966), p. 433.

probabilities of our purchase being in state *A*, *B*, and *C* would "settle down to a set of fixed values" [7]. In this example these values are 0.36, 0.23, and 0.41 for brands *A*, *B*, and *C*, respectively.

The problem of interest to the marketer, however, is to *change* the transition probabilities in ways favorable to his firm's brand. For example, the marketer of brand *A* would ideally like to make the transition probability of state *A* to state *A* approach unity; this can be viewed as increasing the "loyalty" measure. Similarly, he would like to increase the probabilities of customers moving from state *B* to state *A* and state *C* to state A. These are frequently referred to as "attractiveness" measures. Unfortunately, competitors would like to increase *their* respective "loyalty" and "attractiveness" measures.

The upshot of this interplay of competitive strategies is that the transition matrix shown in Table 4.1 rarely remains stable over extended periods of time. Rather, it will reflect the effectiveness of the marketing strategies used by the producers of brands A, B, and C. If the transition matrices are changing over time, however, the application of standard analytical methods becomes much more difficult. Furthermore, in this simple form of the model, we have neglected such considerations as: (a) the time interval between purchase, (b) the amount purchased on each buying occasion, (c) the entry and exit of customers to and from the market, and (d) the placement of new brands on the market. As more realism is introduced into the brand-switching model, it becomes more and more difficult to "solve" by analytical methods.

Simulation Models. Our discussion so far has stressed analytical models or numerical procedures of an iterative type. As could be inferred from our discussion of Markov brand-switching models, however, the opportunity to use analytical techniques declines rapidly if realistic situations are to be modeled. Simulation is a numerical procedure also, but iterative solution procedures are not dealt with in the same way that are linear programming techniques as discussed earlier. Most marketing processes are so complex that realistic models of these processes are not analytically tractable.

Simulation is a term which had been applied to a variety of numerical procedures, including business games, experimental gaming (see Chapter 2), and the modeling of human decision processes (heuristic programming). One subset of simulation techniques that is of particular importance to the marketing researcher is called the Monte Carlo procedure; we describe this technique as an illustration of simulation.

Monte Carlo techniques are essentially experimental sampling methods for modeling systems which are either essentially probabilistic or are deterministic, but can be approximated by a probabilistic process. We shall illustrate the former (most often-used) application. This illustration has been drawn from Green and Tull [90].

Consider a situation in which a firm has a service facility composed of technical personnel whose job it is to provide information for the solution of problems encountered by customers who use the firm's product (heavy machinery). We assume that the weekly demand for service is not known with certainty but can be characterized by a probability distribution which is estimated from historical data. All technical service employees work a 40-hour week and must be paid time and a half for hours worked in excess of this number.

Although vacations are covered by temporary summer employees, we assume that absenteeism represents a pertinent factor in the analysis; that is, the lack of availability of man hours is also characterized by a probability distribution. Finally, we assume that any week's demand for technical service is met by overtime work; that is, we allow no "carry-over" of demand into subsequent weeks.

From the preceding description it is clear that if too few service personnel are maintained, overtime costs will be high. If too many service employees are maintained, "idle" time results. What manning level should be maintained for lowest total weekly costs subject to meeting the conditions stated earlier? (The reader will note the similarity in structure to the "inventory" problem class discussed earlier.)

We might be able to solve this problem analytically if we could characterize the demand and absenteeism distributions mathematically, but for purposes of illustration we show how Monte Carlo might be applied to obtain the solution. Fig. 4.6 shows, respectively, the cumulative probability distribution of demand for service (in terms of weekly manhours) and cumulative probability distribution of lost manhours (due to absenteeism). We assume that these distributions are mutually independent and, over the range of possible manning levels to be considered here, are also independent of manning level. We further assume that the cost per straight time hour C_1 is \$2.50 and the cost per overtime hour C_2 is \$3.75.

With this "data" we can now proceed to work through a sample run of "experience," using a Monte Carlo procedure. We notice that the demand distribution of Fig. 4.6 has a mean of approximately 3675 hours. The distribution of manhours lost due to absenteeism has a mean of approximately 80 hours. On the average then about 3755 hours would be required. In terms of manpower, this means $\frac{3755}{40} \cong 94$ technical service personnel. What would be the average annual cost if 94 men were maintained?

We can approach this problem via Monte Carlo in the following manner. First, we draw two sets of two-digit random numbers, one set related to the demand distribution and one set related to the absenteeism

Table **4.2**   Illustration of Monte Carlo Run Work Force—94 Men

Demand Distribution		Availability Distribution					
R N	Demand	Gross	R N	Absentee-ism	Net	Over-time	Idle Time
(65)	3650	3760	(39)	90	3670	0	20
(03)	3810	3760	(78)	60	3700	110	0
(29)	3710	3760	(01)	170	3590	120	0
(23)	3735	3760	(41)	85	3675	60	0
(40)	3695	3760	(65)	75	3685	10	0
(14)	3750	3760	(37)	95	3665	85	0

distribution and by using the charts of Fig. 4.6 find the appropriate man-hours of demand and lost manhours due to absenteeism of each sampled week. Table 4.2 illustrates the approach under the assumption of a 94-man work force.

Looking at Table 4.2, we note that the first random number (65) results in a simulated demand of 3650 manhours. This is found by following the dotted line to the horizontal axis of the cumulative probability distribution of demand (Fig. 4.6). That is, we drop a perpendicular from the point on the curve which represents the intersection of a horizontal line drawn from the vertical axis (at the value 0.65) to the curve. Simi-

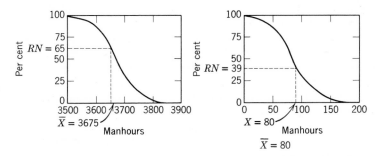

Fig. 4.6   Panel A. Cumulative probability distribution of demand (percentage of weeks in which demand manhours exceed levels noted on horizontal scale). Panel B. Cumulative probability distribution of lost manhours due to absenteeism (percentage of weeks in which lost manhours exceed levels noted on horizontal scale). Reproduced, with permission, from P. E. Green and D. S. Tull, *Research for Marketing Decisions* (Englewood Cliffs, N. J.: Prentice-Hall, 1966), p. 411.

Table **4.3**   Average Weekly Cost as a Function of Manning Level

Technical Service Level (Men)	Average Weekly Fixed Cost	Average Weekly Overtime Cost	Average Weekly Total Cost
97	$9700	$ 2	$9702
96	9600	11	9611
95	9500	35	9535
94	9400	89	9489
93	9300	179	9479
92	9200	300	9500
91	9100	438	9538

larly, the random number (39), representing the first selection from the absenteeism distribution, results in 90 manhours lost due to absenteeism. We subtract these manhours from the gross availability of 3760 manhours (90 × 40) to arrive at a net availability figure.

Notice that in our sample run of "six weeks," only the first week resulted in "available" manhours exceeding "demand" manhours. (In practice, however, we would not stop with a sample of only six weeks.) Table 4.3 shows the results of a Monte Carlo "run" of 150 weeks from which we derived overtime hours and cost associated with manning levels ranging from 91 to 97 men.

As noted from Table 4.3 and Fig. 4.7, our Monte Carlo results showed that a manning level of 93 technical service personnel leads to the lowest average weekly cost of $9,479.

In this simplified illustration we have neglected such considerations as (a) the valuation of "idle" time, (b) seasonal, cyclical, or trend changes in demand, (c) the value of reducing absenteeism, and so on. In more realistic formulations of this problem these factors could be considered explicitly if data were available. Moreover, we could evaluate policies which permitted "carry-over" of technical service demand hours to subsequent weeks. If we desired, we could have determined the sensitivity of the "optimal" manning level to various perturbations in the demand and absenteeism destributions.

In this simplified formulation we assumed that the components of the problem were known (probabilistically) and that the rules for combining these components were also given. Our only concern was to find the numerical consequences of these assumptions. We could increase the reliability of our estimates by making longer Monte Carlo runs, and if so desired, could build a distribution of numerical results by making a

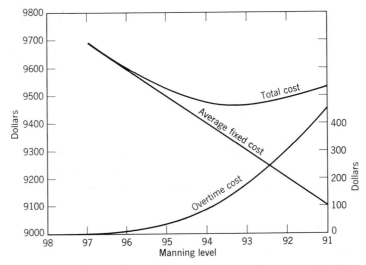

Fig. 4.7   Behavior of average weekly fixed cost, overtime cost and total cost as a function of manning level. Reproduced, with permission, from P. E. Green, and D. S. Tull, *Research for Marketing Decisions* (Englewood Cliffs, N. J.: Prentice-Hall, 1966), p. 413.

series of runs of, say, 150 weeks each. In the illustrative problem such a refinement hardly appears worthwhile. In more complicated problem formulations, however, it may be of interest to report the results of a series of Monte Carlo runs.

As might be gathered from the preceding description, in using Monte Carlo procedures we do not need to be able to characterize the probability distributions by mathematical functions. Rather we use Monte Carlo to reproduce the characteristics of the probabilistic process (whatever form it takes), thus generating a whole distribution of "states of the world." A practical application of Monte Carlo has already been described in our discussion of risk analysis (Chapter 1). We describe additional applications of this and other techniques in the next section of this chapter.

Applications of Models in Marketing
Now that we have discussed some of the conceptual bases of models and various solution techniques, we turn to a description

of some *applications* of model building to marketing. We use the term "applications" advisedly, however. Much of the literature on modeling in marketing discusses models from a general and descriptive point of view. In many cases it is not clear that the models proposed in the literature have actually been applied. Problems of industrial security have also precluded many actual applications from appearing in the literature.

Market planning models

Several models have been proposed for decision making in the general domain of market planning. One of the first corporate-level models, proposed by R. S. Weinberg [181] was the "multiple-factor-break-even" model. Weinberg was interested in the environmental influences on a firm's profits. These environments consist of (a) a general economic activity level insofar as it affects total industry sales; (b) total industry sales in which the firm shares; (c) competitors' actions insofar as they influence the firm's share; (d) the firm's actions in influencing its sales and profits; and (e) the tax situation insofar as it influences the firm's net profits after taxes.

Figure 4.8 shows the interrelationships among the preceding factors. Starting from level A (general economic activity level), we can trace out the effects on industry sales, company sales, and company net profits (before and after taxes) as various relationships are changed. Alternative marketing strategies will have the effect of changing the firm's market share and cost relationships. Weinberg's model provides a means for tracing through the net impact of change for either controlled or uncontrolled variables, once the relationships have been estimated. A principal value of the model is the flexibility it provides for conducting "sensitivity" analyses; that is, tracing through the implications of a variety of assumptions about the influence of various strategies on components of the model.

Another "total systems" model has been developed by J. W. Forrester [71] and his colleagues. This model — dubbed "industrial dynamics" — is essentially a total firm simulation viewed as a set of flows of information, material, manpower, capital equipment, and money.

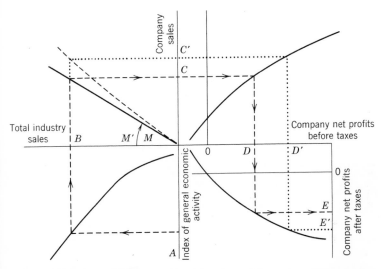

Fig. 4.8 The company's general economic activity–net profits complex. Reproduced, with permission, from R. S. Weinberg, "Management Science and Marketing Strategy," in *Marketing and the Computer,* W. Alderson and S. J. Shapiro (eds.) (Englewood Cliffs, N. J.: Prentice-Hall, 1963), p. 98–127.

Figure 4.9 illustrates a set of time series related to the advertising process, as characterized by Forrester. Assuming a sudden (and "permanent") change in demand, the pool of prospective customers and retail sales will rise. Factory sales will, it is also assumed, rise more rapidly as distribution pipelines are filled. If we further assume that advertising is budgeted as a constant fraction of sales, the chart indicates that this variable will increase, later dip, and then rise again. Finally, the customer's advertising awareness (assumed to follow advertising expenditures) will show the pattern indicated.

All the assumptions of this illustration, of course, are open to question. Forrester's contribution shows their interdependence and time-related aspects. The effort involved in building a "total model" of the firm is immense. Most of the reported work in industrial dynamics has been expository in nature. Nevertheless, the implications of the approach are interesting insofar as they demonstrate

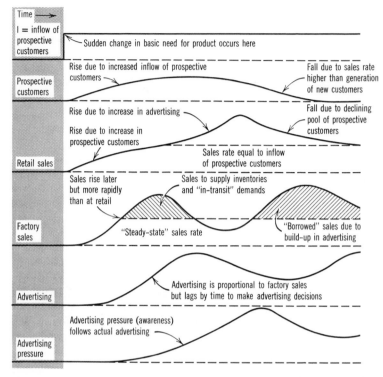

Fig. 4.9   Permanent increase in demand. Reproduced, with permission, from J. W. Forrester, "Advertising: A Problem in Industrial Dynamics," *Harvard Business Review,* **37,** (March–April 1959), pp. 100–110.

some of the potential dangers involved in "decoupling" advertising decisions from other components of the firm's operations.

Sales effort models

The construction of models for dealing with sales effort decisions — advertising, personal selling effort, merchandising — appears to have been a favorite preoccupation of management scientists. Most of these models have been concerned with (a) total budget determination, and (b) allocation of the total among products, territories, and media. (No attempt is made here to present an exhaustive listing of the models.)

The design of models for budgeting advertising goes back at least to the early fifties. Early model-building efforts drew upon the marginal analysis of economic theory and solution techniques of the calculus [58].

In the *allocation* of the total budget (among areas, media, products, etc.) the model [139] also involved utilization of the calculus and Lagrange multipliers. Although solution techniques differed in the various models, they followed essentially the same structure, that is, the models were static and deterministic. Little or no attention was paid to the problems of measuring the appropriate response functions; rather, a response function was chosen that "looked realistic" and was "mathematically tractable."

An interesting illustration of one empirically based model for dealing with advertising effectiveness is the work of Vidale and Wolfe [177]. They were able to develop a three-parameter model consisting of a sales decay constant, a saturation factor, and a response constant for measuring sales response to promotion and, ultimately, for making decisions regarding total budget determination and its allocation.

A noteworthy feature of this model was that its parameters were estimated from empirical data. Figure 4.10 shows, for example, the sales history of an unpromoted product. We note that sales are decreasing exponentially. By analyzing several different products the authors were able to develop numerical values for the "sales decay" constant. Similarly, numerical values were obtained for the saturation factor (the practical limit on sales generated by a particular campaign) and the response constant (sales generated per advertising dollar). The authors state that their model has been able to describe experimental data with reasonable accuracy and that the model has been used to answer such questions as: (a) advertising effort required to sustain sales at a predetermined level, (b) the sales generated by a short but intensive campaign, and (c) allocation of the total budget over products, territories, etc.

Through the interest of large advertising agencies, allocation models were extended to problems of *media mix* determination. Although technical details on these models are sparse, it appears that mathematical programming techniques (linear or convex) are

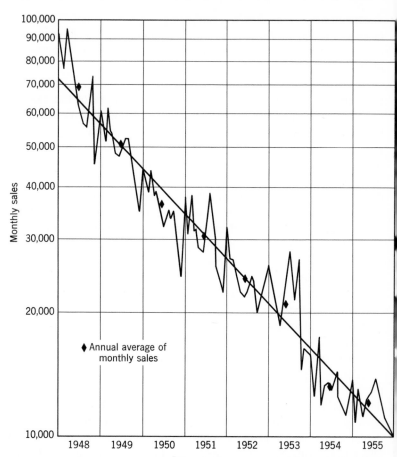

Fig. 4.10   Unpromoted product *A*—sales history. Reproduced, with permission, from M. L. Vidale and H. B. Wolfe, "An Operations Research Study of Sales Response to Advertising," *Operations Research,* **5** (June 1957), pp. 370–381.

representative of the class of solution procedures which are being used [24, 64, 116]. Efforts have also been expended on simulation models of media effectiveness [22].

Some researchers have become attracted to "limited objective" approaches [39] where intermediate variables such as exposure ratings and recall are substituted for sales data. Usually missing, however, are the rules of transformation by which these intermediate variables are to be translated into sales. Also frequently missing are the appropriate cost data. Unfortunately, such approaches cannot provide answers to the economic problem of how much to spend on advertising, even assuming that subdecisions are "loosely coupled" enough to justify solving the problem on a component-by-component basis.

Model builders have also entered the domain of *personal selling* and the evaluation of technical services and salesman compensation plans. An early application of operations research to the determination of optimal-call frequency of salesmen was reported by Ackoff [3]. Ackoff's findings indicated that a considerable reduction could be made in call frequency without adversely affecting the firm's (General Electric's Lamp Division) sales. In another study, which used a planned experimental design in which call rates were varied, researchers were able to develop procedures for determining the optimal balance between customer "holding" and "conversion" effort. Based on these results, the authors were also able to provide recommendations on total sales force size.

Modeling efforts have also been applied to the evaluation of such diverse activities as salesman compensation plans [68], technical services [156], product guarantee policies [95], and the selection of potential accounts for personal sales calls [130].

Pricing models

In contrast to the large amount of modeling effort being undertaken in the promotion and personal selling areas, relatively few models have been developed for making pricing decisions. Although economic theorists have had a lot to say about how firms *should* set price (application of the marginal analysis), the problems encountered in the empirical determination of price-volume relationships have seriously restricted applications of the marginal analysis.

Most of the model-building activity has been concentrated on various measurement devices — regression analysis, designed experiments — as means for estimating appropriate demand relationships. Once demand and cost functions are estimated, application of the marginal analysis (using techniques of the calculus) becomes fairly straightforward.

Green [7] has reported an application of decision theory to

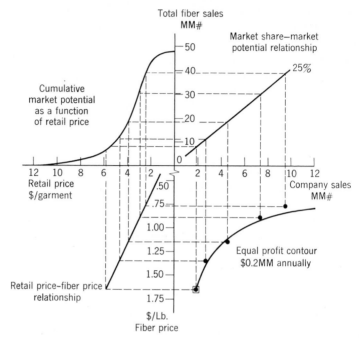

Fig. 4.11   Price-volume relationships in market *A* (first approximation). Reproduced, with permission, from W. Alderson and P. E. Green, *Planning and Problem Solving in Marketing* (Homewood, Ill.: Richard D. Irwin, 1964), p. 255.

pricing problems faced by a larger producer of textile fibers. Figure 4.11 shows an illustration of the approach. Assume that the fiber is selling currently at $1.65 per pound to primary users (spinning and weaving mills who, in turn, sell the cloth to garment manufacturers). The firm's equal profit contour can be arrived at by tracing along the dotted line. The lower right-hand quadrant shows how. If the price of the fiber were reduced to, say, $1.15 per pound, it is estimated that garments containing the fiber could be produced to sell for $4.00 retail and over. Assuming that the firm would keep approximately the market share already being obtained in higher retail price brackets, we note that company sales (at 4.5 million pounds) would be sufficient to yield profits equal to those currently being earned at the higher-price figure. Sales beyond 4.5 million pounds would of course place the firm on a higher-profit contour.

Of course the foregoing comments merely pertain to a component-by-component description of break-even considerations. The problem is to ascertain the effects of (a) independent actions of various fiber processors on cloth and garment prices, and (b) market share achievement in lower retail price brackets, on actual (rather than break-even) profits. The author goes on to show how these variables can be incorporated in the analysis.

Green [81] also has described an application of Bayesian decision theory to a problem of industrial product pricing, involving such variables as competitors' reactions and short-term as well as the longer-term impact of lower prices on changes in industry capacity. Cook and Halbert [41] have reported an empirical application of demand analysis in the determination of optimal pricing schedules for a gas utility.

Model builders have also been active in the area of competitive bidding strategy. Friedman [77] has discussed one type of statistical technique for coping with this problem and Christenson [50] has described several modeling approaches to the problem of bidding for corporate securities.

Product decision models

Several models have been proposed for dealing with various decisions related to new product development and modification. Most of these studies have been concerned with the screening of new product ideas and the evaluation of product candidates.

O'Meara [140] employed a type of "profile" analysis for screening product candidates for possible application. Essentially, O'Meara employs a decision theoretic approach in which experienced evaluators are asked to estimate subjective probabilities that various criteria will be met by the product candidate under consideration. Figure 4.12 shows an illustration of the approach. For example, suppose the evaluator wishes to rate the attractiveness of product X with respect to "marketability." The subfactors comprising marketability are listed in the first column of the figure. The second column lists the "importance weight" assigned to each subfactor. The evaluator is asked to enter in columns 3 through 7

Fig. 4.12 Example of the use of an evaluation sheet. Reproduced, with permission, from J. T. O'Meara, Jr., "Selecting Profitable Products," *Harvard Business Review*, **39** (January–February 1961), pp. 83–89.

Proposed product: Product X
Factor: Marketability
Evaluated by: John Smith

1	2	3		4		5		6		7		8	9
		Very Good (10)		Good (8)		Average (6)		Poor (4)		Very Poor (2)		Total	Subfactor Evaluation
Subfactor	Subfactor Weight	EP	EV	EP	EV	EP	EV	EP	EV	EP	EV	EV	EV (Col. 2 × Col. 8)
Relative to present distribution channels	1.0	0.1	1.0	0.2	1.6	0.5	3.0	0.2	0.8	—	—	6.4	6.4
Relative to present product lines	1.0	0.1	1.0	0.2	1.6	0.4	2.4	0.2	0.8	0.1	0.2	6.0	6.0
Quality/price relationship	3.0	0.3	3.0	0.4	3.2	0.2	1.2	0.1	0.4	—	—	7.8	23.4
Number of sizes and grades	1.0	0.1	1.0	0.2	1.6	0.5	3.0	0.2	0.8	—	—	6.4	6.4
Merchandisability	2.0	0.5	5.0	0.4	3.2	0.1	0.6	—	—	—	—	8.8	17.6
Effects on sale of present products	2.0	—	—	0.2	1.6	0.5	3.0	0.3	1.2	—	—	5.8	11.6
	10.0									Total factor value			71.4

NOTE: *EP* = estimated probability as judged by management; *EV* = expected value computed by multiplying the rating's numerical value by the estimated probability.

the chance that product X will be "very good" . . . "very poor" with respect to each subfactor. Expected values are then obtained by multiplying each probability weight by the weight of each subfactor. Finally, in column 9 the evaluator multiplies each subfactor weight by its expected value and a total index is obtained. O'Meara then goes on to discuss the computation of additional measures — payback index, long range profitability table, etc. Essentially, the procedure is similar to that just described in the sense that subjective probabilities are combined with various cash flow measures to yield a set of indexes for making interproduct comparisons.

Some of the characteristics of statistical decision theory are also being applied to the preparation of cash flow analyses for new product candidates [7, 103]. Learner [124] and De Voe [53] have explored the applicability of a network model for evaluating new-product ventures. Kuehn and Day [121] have described a model, using behavioral scaling, for evaluating product quality as a guide to the modification of existing products as well as for determining the functional features of new products which are most likely to be desired by the consumer.

Critical path techniques have also been applied to new-product scheduling and related activities. Christensen and Greene [49] describe an activity sequence involving such considerations as financial analysis, market testing, package design, and advertising campaign preparation. Figure 4.13 depicts the sequence for the example that they developed. Although time and cost information are not shown here, the authors also describe computer procedures for developing "trade-offs" between completion time and project cost.

Channel, distribution, and location models

Management scientists have also devoted effort toward the construction of models of distribution systems. For reporting purposes these models can be classed as channel, physical distribution, and location models.

Balderston [11] and Balderston and Hoggatt [12] have been very active in the development of channel models. In the first article Balderston discusses some of the theoretical aspects of the relationship of distributors to producers and buyers. In the second

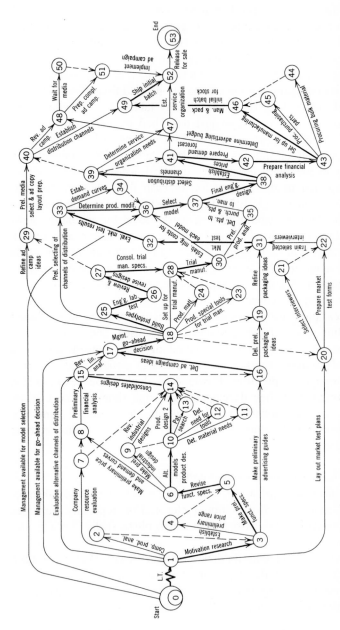

Fig. 4.13 Arrow diagram for launching product XYZ. Reproduced, with permission, from B. M. Christensen and J. R. Greene, "Planning, Scheduling, and Controlling the Launching of a New Product Via CPM," in *Marketing and the Computer*, W. Alderson and S. J. Shapiro (eds.) (Englewood Cliffs, N. J.: Prentice-Hall, 1963), p. 188.

article Balderston and Hoggatt describe an extensive simulation of the Pacific Coast lumber industry, including manufacturers, wholesalers, and retailers. The authors' motivation was to describe interrelationships among firms in the industry. The model could also be used, however, to predict changes in such variables as prices and market structure in response to variations in lumber demand.

An early application of regression analysis to the problem of rating the relative efficiency of various distributors has been reported by Varnum [175]. The model takes into account such factors as population, general retail sales, and effective buying income of each sales territory.

The area of physical distribution has received a lot of attention by management scientists, which is not surprising in view of the comparatively well-structured nature of these problems. Several models [32, 131, 143] have been proposed for handling various aspects of inventory levels, shipment schedules, and transportation cost.

Kuehn and Hamburger [122] describe an interesting model for determining the geographical pattern of warehouse location, based on a balancing of transportation cost, operation cost, and the incremental profits associated with increases in the speed of delivery to the customer. The authors develop a "heuristic" (systematic rule-of-thumb) program, a flow diagram of which is shown in Fig. 4.14. The program proceeds sequentially by locating warehouses one at a time until no additional units can be added without increasing total costs. The program then examines modifications of the first approach either by deleting warehouses considered in the first step or by shifting them among locations.

Site location problems (retail shopping centers, supermarkets, etc.) have also been modeled by management scientists. For the most part, model builders have employed techniques — so-called gravity models — drawing from the regional sciences. The proposed models [123, 167, 183] typically consider population masses and distances of potential sites from existing shopping centers. Various refinements covering such variables as driving time and discretionary income are introduced in an effort to make the models more realistic.

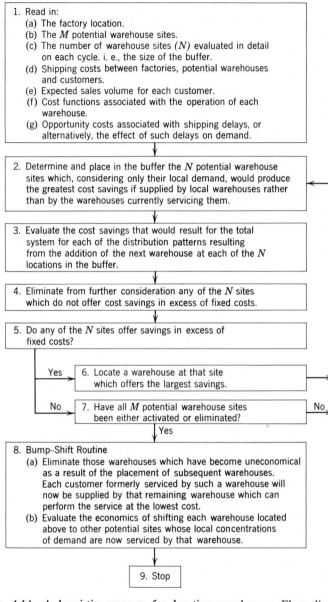

Fig. 4.14 A heuristic program for locating warehouses. Flow diagram. Reproduced, with permission, from A. A. Kuehn and M. J. Hamburger, "A Heuristic Program for Locating Warehouses," *Management Science,* **9** (July 1963), pp. 643–666.

Buyer behavior models

We have already discussed (Chapter 2) various behavioral models for explaining buyer behavior. A particularly popular behavioral "model" as viewed by the management scientist is the Markov brand-switching model. Several articles dealing with this type of model have been reported [59, 72, 96, 120, 128, 169].

The dearth of "practical applications" of Markov switching models has been described in an evaluative article by Ehrenberg [63]. Although the original formulations of the model have been altered to relax some of the restrictive assumptions [108], the fact remains that most applications of the Markov model to date have involved their use as "diagnostic" rather than predictive devices. That is, many of the mathematical properties of the "stationary" model — steady-state solutions, rate of approach to equilibrium — are *not* relevant if the transition probabilities themselves are changing. Simulation may be useful, however, in dealing with the less tractable (but more realistic) nonstationary Markov processes.

Fewer modeling efforts have been devoted to industrial purchasing decisons and to choice making by distributors (for example, agents, wholesalers, retailers). A recent attempt to model the industrial buying process has been reported by Webster [180], however. He discusses a conceptual framework involving (a) problem recognition, (b) assignment of buying responsibility, (c) search, and (d) choice, for analyzing industrial purchase decisions.

Current State of the Art of Model Building in Marketing

In the preceding section of the chapter we have tried to give the reader some idea of the diversity of model-building efforts in marketing; even so, our brief discussion of problem classes, solution techniques, and "applications" has hardly been intensive or exhaustive. Moreover, with few exceptions we have refrained from making critical comments about the proposed models in terms of their predictive efficacy, assumption structure, and data requirements.

In this section we first discuss some of the general limitations of present "prescriptive" models and the practical problems associated with the implementation of these models. Next we describe some of the "human" problems that have arisen between manager and model builder in the process of implementing the model builder's recommendations.

Technical limitations of current models

As indicated earlier, the mathematical modeling of marketing systems has involved, for the most part, prescriptive models, the ultimate purpose of which is to assist the researcher in making a recommendation that some course of action is "better" than others under consideration. Once the descriptive part of the model has been constructed, a variety of optimization techniques — the calculus, mathematical programming — can be used to solve the model.

The major problem facing model builders in marketing is a *lack of understanding of the descriptive part of the model.* It is one thing to *postulate* a response function of sales to changes in advertising expenditures and then solve the model. It is quite another thing to *measure* the response function and arrive at a realistic description of sales behavior with respect to advertising changes. As stated in the preceding section, the pioneering model builders were content to "pick a functional relationship that looked reasonable" and then solve the model on the basis of little or no data.

Our current lack of understanding of marketing relationships — and, hence, knowledge of the appropriate predictive aspects of the model — constitutes a major limitation to the applications of current models. In our judgment, realistic models in marketing will have to take into account, to an increasing extent, the problems of interaction and system instability. We discuss these limitations in terms of (a) interaction phenomena and (b) nonstationary characteristics of marketing systems.

Interaction Phenomena in Marketing. We have already commented on the many courses of action typically available to the firm in selecting, for example, the appropriate marketing mix — advertising, personal selling, pricing, distribution, marketing and technical service. Most of the models we discussed earlier have decoupled one part of the problem from other parts. We have a plethora of *advertising* effectiveness models, but the effectiveness of advertising may, of course, depend on what the firm is doing with regard to other variables in the marketing mix.

Most of the models discussed make either no assumptions or very naive ones about competitors' actions. How "optimal" is a so-called optimization model if competitors are using *similar* techniques? This question has received virtually no attention at all. Rather, all the models we have discussed suffer from the danger of "incomplete" optimization, although *full* comprehension of a system is an unattainable ideal. It would be preferable to increase the realism of models to encompass variables not heretofore included, or at least to develop policies that are not highly sensitive to factors not under the firm's control.

Some activities under way on the model-building front are addressed to the problems enumerated above. Firms are using to an increasing extent statistically designed field experiments in which components of the sales effort mix are systematically varied over space or time for the purpose of estimating the response "surface" of sales (and/or intermediate variables, such as awareness and recall, which are assumed to be correlated with sales) to changes in amount and type of sales effort. Such "intangible" variables as advertising quality [92] are also receiving attention. In short, current activity appears to be emphasizing *systematic measurement procedures* for determining response functions under a variety of conditions. Controlled experimentation (and regression analysis) represents a major activity on the part of firms who have passed the "naive" stage of model formulation.

Less work is being done on the development of interactive models which explore the "optimality" of various models under varying environmental conditions with regard to competitor, distributor, and consumer reactions. There is reason to believe, however, that computer simulation will be used to an increasing extent in exploring the "robustness" of various models under alternative environmental conditions.

In summary, the model builder has started to recognize the limitations of previous optimization techniques, the need to establish functional relationships ("well-behaved," in a mathematical sense, or not) through controlled experimentation, and the value of exploring the behavior of the model under a variety of environmental conditions.

Ultimately, of course, we would like to *understand* buying behavior, not merely measure its sales effects through controlled experimentation. Markov process models, with all their limitations, have been proposed as a model of brand switching. Other models [115] have been cited as well. Although less progress appears to have been made in this area of research, current activity in behavioral scaling and experimental gaming may hopefully shed light on the development of explanatory models.

Nonstationary characteristics of marketing systems

Another major problem facing the model builder in marketing is the (seeming) lack of stability of relationships over time. (We have already encountered this problem in our discussion of some of the criticisms that have been leveled against Markov brand-switching models.) Will sales-advertising relationships which have been measured by time-consuming and costly experimentation be stable enough to persist into the next period(s) when, presumably, the firm will act on the experimental findings?

It has often been said that marketing is characterized by instability; that, in fact, it is the objective of advertising managers, sales managers, and new product managers to upset the status quo and, hopefully thereby, increase the firm's market share and profit position. Can the model builder ever hope to predict the effects of courses of action in the light of policies dedicated to change?

All prediction, however, is based on the assumption of *some* type of stability in the system under study. The terms "static" and "dynamic" are relative. For example, a trend equation which predicts that sales in the next period will be 10 per cent higher than this period's sales is making a "dynamic" forecast; however, the analyst assumes that the values of the parameters in the model being used to predict sales are stable over the forecast period.

Similarly, a researcher may design a model for predicting changes in the transition probabilities of a Markov process model. If so, the transition probabilities are "nonstationary" but not the model being used to predict them. What the researcher has done is to develop a "supermodel" for predicting changes in "lower-level" models. The point is that the model builder is free to choose the level of the process which he assumes to be stable. Such "super" and "super-super" decision rules can characterize processes that at lower levels, appear to be rapidly changing in some unpredictable manner.

This is not to say, of course, that the construction of such higher-level models is now or will ever be an easy task. It is to say, however, that the argument that "everything is changing too fast to analyze" is not necessarily correct. If the process exhibits instability at *all* levels which the analyst can conceive, there is little to be gained in trying to predict the system's output. It would be akin to trying to predict the next digit in a random number sequence. Fortunately, we "have faith" that *most* systems, at some level, exhibit sufficient stability for us to make useful predictions; finding this level, of course, may be another matter.

Interaction of manager and model builder

Many arguments have been advanced to "explain" why greater use has not been made of mathematical models in marketing. In the preceding section we have tried to explain some of the technical problems in currently formulated models. A second class of problems [29] may be classed as "administrative" and are concerned with the relationship between manager and model builder.

We have all heard some of these arguments: "The model builder (manager) doesn't understand the manager (model builder)"; "The manager is afraid of the specialist"; "The specialist is too much interested in the technique — not the real problem." The illustrations are almost endless; so are the bromides which have been put forth: "The model builder (manager) should learn to communicate better with the manager (model builder)"; "More time should be taken in formulating the problem and controlling the solution," and so on.

The fact remains, however, that the relationship of model builders to marketing managers (or to "traditional" marketing researchers) has been beset with problems. Management scientists have made the most (technical) progress in the *evaluative* (choice) phase of problem solving. Much less is known about the other components of the process: problem definition, development of courses of action, and implementation and control of the solution. Some researchers [145] have taken as serious problems for research such activities as "implementation" of research results.

Behavioral experiments are under way in a number of educational institutions whose purpose is to develop understanding of the behavioral characteristics and communications processes which influence receptivity to recommendations.

It is our guess that much more research will be devoted to such aspects of problem solving as problem recognition, formulation, and solution implementation. This is in keeping with the growing role of the behavioral scientist in management research. We discuss this topic in more detail in the next chapter.

Summary

In this chapter we have introduced the reader to mathematical (with little of the accompanying mathematics) modeling of marketing systems. After first discussing some of the problems attendant with the modeling of marketing phenomena, we listed some of the major problem classes for which models have been proposed. As we saw, the model builder's preoccupation is with the *structural* properties of systems; this point of view can be very useful in the attack on problems of widely varying content.

We next discussed some of the major techniques — the calculus, mathematical programming, simulation — that have been used to find solutions to models. We then listed (with little critical comment at that point) a variety of modeling approaches to marketing problems which have appeared in the literature. Unfortunately, little is known about actual applications of these (or other) models [29].

We then discussed some of the principal technical limitations which apply rather generally to current marketing models and described some of the research which is currently being undertaken to improve the "realism" of marketing models. We concluded this chapter with some comments on the human problems associated with the interaction of manager and model builder and current research on this set of problems.

5 Future Developments in Marketing Research

Introduction

Up to this point our discussion of recent developments in marketing research methods and techniques has been largely reportorial and has rested on three major premises:

1. The activity of marketing research is assuming increasing importance to managerial decision making as the executive's *need* for improved information and understanding of marketing phenomena continues to expand.
2. The *methodological potential* of marketing research procedures is being significantly increased by techniques drawn originally from the behavioral, statistical, and mathematical disciplines.
3. Responsibility for the *continued development* of these newer techniques is being assumed more and more by the marketing researcher. Marketing research personnel are not only learning these techniques but are also contributing toward their extension.

In this chapter we discuss the types of *future* research in marketing that we feel will command the attention of the "new breed" of marketing research specialists and the implications of these new activities for the practice, staffing, administration, and training of marketing researchers (and, to a large extent, *the training of managers,* as well).

In this chapter our discussion becomes much more speculative. Still, these speculations are based on an existing bank of evidence which would appear to lend some credence to our extrapolations.

151

We first review some of the major gaps in our knowledge of marketing processes and their implications for both basic and applied research in the future.

Next we discuss the implications of this newer research on the administration and training of marketing research personnel in the future. If our speculations are correct, it would appear that rather marked changes will appear in the organization and skills required in this activity. Moreover, preparation for many of these changes can be profitably started now.

Present Problems and Future Research in Marketing

In our judgment, the new developments — decision theory, behavorial techniques, statistical experiments, and mathematical models — described in earlier chapters are here to stay. Not that they are without limitations, but present limitations provide opportunities for continued research and improvement.

In this section of the chapter we discuss some of the major limitations of the current state of the art. Next we speculate about the types of research that will be forthcoming from both "basic" and "applied" marketing research groups.

Limitations of the new techniques

In the overview material of Chapter 1 we asserted that the Bayesian model of cost-versus-value-of-information will provide a unifying framework for appraising the value of marketing research and a useful guide for the allocation of research resources among competing activities. To our knowledge, very few companies have adopted this framework. Part of this lag in application is to be expected on the grounds that the diffusion of new methodology often takes several years to appear in routine application. Aside from this, however, some very real methodological problems remain. First, we still know relatively little about the validity and reliability of prior information supplied by "predictive experts," that is, the information incorporated into the Bayesian model as "prior" probabilities. Second, we still know very little about how organizations form goals, develop trade-offs among conflicting goals, and how stable the value measures derived from these deliberations remain over time.

In Chapter 2 we discussed attitudinal scaling and experimental approaches to the measurement and prediction of choice behavior. Despite the large number of "psychophysical" techniques which have been developed, relatively little has been done to validate verbal responses by behavioral measures. Moreover, we still know relatively little about multidimensional scaling, the stability of personality attributes over time, and the influence of situational variables on consumer choice. For example, although various attempts in advertising research have been made to measure such variables as "awareness," "recall," and "impact," we still know little about how these intermediate variables are related to sales.

In Chapter 3 we discussed experimental design and multivariate techniques. Although statistically designed experiments represent a way to develop appropriate response functions to changes in amount and kind of sales effort, here again application of these procedures is time consuming and expensive. Are the measurements worth the cost of data collection and are the phenomena sufficiently stable to permit useful predictions? With respect to multivariate analysis, most current techniques assume linear relationships among variables. Are these sufficiently accurate approximations to the actual relationships among large masses of behavioral data?

In Chapter 4 we discussed prescriptive models as related to marketing decisions in promotion, pricing, product development, channel selection, physical distribution, and site location. Most of the current models make simplifying assumptions about competitive behavior and the influence of a firm's other courses of action on the decision process being studied. Can we develop more "comprehensive" models that treat simultaneously the influence of several decision variables (on the part of the firm, competitors, and distributors) on sales and profits?

We believe that these questions are symptomatic of the kinds of research that are needed and will be undertaken as knowledge about the current state of the art is diffused among many interested groups. In some cases the research will be conducted by university-based research groups and other types of nonprofit institutions. In other instances the type of research needed can only be performed by research groups in business firms dealing with data and problems from the real market place.

Before speculating on more specific methodological research

that will be undertaken in the future, by either basic or applied groups, it is useful to place the development of current technology in historical perspective. If anything, this "trend analysis" of methodological developments should provide some insight into the speed and breadth of research progress in marketing.

Historical development of research methodology in marketing

It seems fair to say that methodological development in marketing research is proceeding at an increasing rate. Lipstein [126], in a recent paper, has commented upon the rapid pace of technical developments in marketing. Using the advertising agency business as an illustration, he has listed the years in which important methodological innovations were first "applied" (bearing in mind that application may well refer to trial usage only).

Figure 5.1 shows the results of Lipstein's investigation. As can be noted from the chart, such services as the Nielsen store audit and opinion polls had their start in the thirties. In the forties and fifties many of the techniques described in earlier chapters (probability sampling, regression and correlation techniques, multivariate analysis, behavioral scaling) received (at least some) attention in advertising. In the sixties, operations research techniques — mathematical programming, decision theory, etc. — have made some impression.

As Lipstein suggests, the traditional advertising (marketing) researcher has been joined by a variety of specialists — statisticians, sociologists, mathematicians, economists, psychologists — and their impact has been increasingly felt on the design and conduct of research investigations.

Ackoff [4] has also commented on the changes taking place in the application of management science to business. He indicates that early efforts tended to be restricted to specific types of problems — inventory, allocation, queuing, etc. — and to tactical decision making levels. Ackoff suggests that efforts of management scientists will be devoted, to a growing extent, to the problems arising in organization structure and communication. He cites "decomposition" programming methods as a case in point for tackling higher-level problems on a piecemeal basis which, nevertheless, permits aggregation of solutions to subparts in a manner consistent with higher-level objectives.

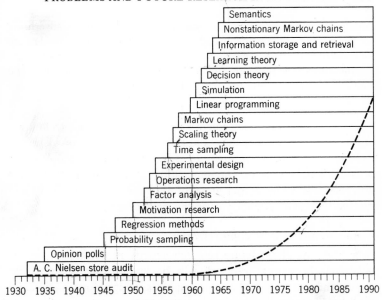

Fig. 5.1 The growth rate of innovation in advertising-marketing research. Reproduced, with permission, from B. Lipstein, "Prospects for the Managerial Sciences in Advertising," paper presented at the American Meeting of the Institute of Management Sciences, Dallas, Texas (February 1966).

Our own study of the changes taking place in the behavioral and management sciences leads to a view compatible with those expressed by Lipstein and Ackoff. As Green [83] has indicated,

. . . the techniques of management science seem to have made the most progress in substantive areas which are typified by a short time horizon, and by repetitive problems of choices among well-structured alternatives in the satisfaction of a well-defined figure of merit. Many of the past and current techniques involve normative decision making under closed, stationary, deterministic, or well-defined probabilistic systems represented by simple objective functions, e.g., cash flow or net profits. But contrast these characteristics with the open, dynamic adaptive systems of marketing. For example, several analytical models have been proposed for making promotional-mix decisions. For the most part, these models ignore the interaction of promotional decisions with other actions taken by the firm, actions taken by competitors, exogenous changes in consumer demand, and so on. Not only do the models assume a large dose of *ceteris paribus,* but the alternative courses of action (types of promotional media, vehicles within medium, frequency of stimulus, advertising theme, etc.) are highly aggregated. Neglected in most of the models are such considerations as the cost of uncertainty, the cost of collecting data on the unknown response functions, the anticipated reliability and stability of the data, and the means of adapting the model to deal with changes in the relevant parameters.

In our judgment, management and behavioral science techniques are coming "closer together" as a variety of points of view and techniques are being brought to bear on common problems in organizational structure, communication, and problem solving. We now describe some of the areas of research which, we feel, will receive increased attention over the next decade.

Future trends in marketing research

In speculating about future research activity in marketing, we believe that behavioral research will be less distinguishable from management science research as emphasis swings to more strategic-level problem applications and to the study of *other* components of the problem solving process — problem recognition, goal formation, implementation, and control of selected acts. Heretofore, most research has concentrated on the evaluative (or choice) component.

With regard to specific research areas, we believe that future research [84] will be devoted, to an increasing extent, to the following:

1. *Value theory.* Extension of formal theories to deal with multi-dimensional scaling, goal stability, and intragroup goal formation; further effort devoted to stochastic preference theory.
2. *Sequential, adaptive models.* Extensions of statistical decision theory and mathematical programming to deal with dynamic, multistage problems under uncertainty.
3. *Gaming and interactive models.* Increased efforts to model larger, more complex processes where courses of action are interrelated and where nonlinearities predominate.
4. *Investigation of predictive experts and rules of thumb.* Increased emphasis on models which include parameters estimated by "predictive experts" (and models for validating the

experts' predictive accuracy and reliability) and investigation of current rule-of-thumb versus prescriptive procedures in making "optimal" decisions.

5. *Models of search, implementation, and control.* Extensions of current evaluative models, to deal with the design, implementation, and control of courses of action.

6. *Behavioral aspects of decision making and conflict.* Increased research on the development of behavioral theories of the firm and the relationship of the firm to its environment.

7. *Model validation.* Greater efforts devoted to experimental design, on-line simulation, search routines, and sequential modification of models.

8. *Total systems simulation.* Development of larger models, encompassing all components of the marketing mix.

9. *Joint optimization models.* Using modeling techniques that extend to the producer-distributor-customer sequence, in the effort to assign inventory levels, distribution arrangements, etc., in such a way as to produce lower costs for the *entire* sequence. (Such models could be used as a "marketing service" which indicates the potential gains to be made through mutual cooperation of producer, distributor, and consumer.)

10. *Study of model optimality in interactive systems.* Investigation of the properties of "optimal" models when competitors employ similar techniques and interaction is present.

Although this list is not exclusive or exhaustive, it does suggest an increasing need to model larger, interactive systems composed of relationships which are mainly behavioral. If our "forecasts" are borne out, it seems clear that existing data collection and computational procedures will likewise undergo marked changes.

Data Collection Procedures. With growing emphasis on the study of more comprehensive systems, present data banks need to be substantially modified and enlarged. Much attention has been given to so-called "marketing intelligence" systems [110] which embrace many of the data requirements discussed in earlier chapters.

In the next 20 years Lipstein [126] envisions that computerized information storage and retrieval systems will be commonplace in the advertising agency business. Not only will media and standard service data be stored in these systems, but historical advertising campaign data (for both the firm and its competitors) will be part of the data bank. The media research man will have available continuously updated rates for each medium as well as basic data on reach, frequency, and the demographic and socioeconomic characteristics of the medium's audience as input to a media simulator for testing alternative allocations of media expenditures.

The tabulation and analysis of standard research questionnaires will be fully automated and the results stored in computer files. In addition, store audit techniques will probably undergo substantial changes by having consumer purchases recorded on cash register computers, ultimately to become input data for market simulators. Lipstein speculates that even the "creative" process of advertising copy preparation may be aided by using a computer to search for interesting combinations of appeals from information on customer awareness, preferences, and switching characteristics, in a manner not unlike the way engineers already use computers to design production equipment, bridges, and, indeed, other computers.

If some of these comments sound far-fetched, it is significant to note that market simulators already exist [157], although not on the scale envisioned by Lipstein. Also, the use of central computers with satellite consoles is already a reality.

We would speculate that the marketing departments of agency sponsors will likewise develop data systems, simulators, and the like on a scale comparable to that forecasted for advertising agencies. One of the major advantages of attempts to develop *explicit* models of marketing systems is that attention is focused on the *appropriate data* that must be obtained to make the models operational. For example, some of the recent work in adaptive models [127] suggests that promotional effectiveness models will have a built-in mechanism to specify both "optimal" current promotional expenditures and the field experiments to be conducted in order to keep the model updated for future periods.

Data Processing. Hand in hand with the gathering of data goes the manipulation, summarization, and analysis associated with converting it into usable form for both researcher and manager. Several developments of interest to marketing researchers of the future are already under way.

Much progress has been made in the development of simplified languages by which the user can communicate with the machine. A variety of algebraic and simulation languages have already been developed, and considerable advances are expected to be made along these lines.

Information display devices have long passed the curiosity stage. Automatic plotters and various display devices are currently a reality. In behavioral experiments, for example, the researcher can record subject responses directly on computer tape. Moreover, experimental programs already exist which enable the researcher to "test out" various hypotheses on the data by merely using a console to key in various instructions, thus permitting maximum flexibility in data manipulation.

Research in large probabilistic information processing systems is also a current reality. Edwards and Phillips [62], for example, have been exploring the possibilities of developing large probabilistic information processing systems for the continuous updating of military intelligence. Human experts supply data inputs to a master console, and the likelihood of various hypotheses about adversaries' intentions being true is continuously updated by the computer. Extensions of this approach (which utilizes Bayesian decision theory) to business intelligence systems seem not only possible but likely.

In all probability business accounting systems also will be modified to take into account such concepts as "opportunity costs" (penalties associated with the *failure* to take certain courses of action). We might also speculate, with some justification, that "managers of information" will become part of the top executive elite of the future.

In short, we feel that *current* research activities provide a meaningful basis for making some of the "prognostications" cited. Developments in technology will surely affect the role of marketing research of the future, and the implications of this changed role on the organization and administration of this activity will be significant.

Implications for the Administration of Marketing Research

If we grant the plausibility of the preceding speculations about continued innovation in the methodology of marketing research, it is apparent that these developments portend significant changes in the staffing and organization of this activity. These changes, which we will consider in turn, can be classified as follows:

1. Formal education and continuing training programs for marketing research personnel and marketing management.
2. Growing involvement of line managers in marketing research problem formulation and model validation.
3. The emergence of the research generalist and more centralized decision making authority.

Education of the marketing researcher and marketing manager

A useful starting place from which to appraise the changing nature of education in marketing is the business school. From the changes taking place in business school curricula and teaching methods, it is reasonable to suppose that tomorrow's marketing executives will be very much aware of the techniques discussed in the earlier chapters.

Significant changes have already taken place in most of the nation's leading schools of business. First, business school faculties are becoming increasingly active in basic research on the managerial process. Many faculty members are devoting a substantial portion of their time to the development and extension of many of the techniques reported here. Marketing faculties now include specialists in quantitative methods and various disciplines representative of the behavioral sciences. This augmentation of traditional skills is being manifested in the increasing variety of research projects being conducted by marketing faculty members.

In fairly recent years two new professional journals, *The Journal of Advertising Research* and *The Journal of Marketing Research,* have appeared. The content of both reflects many of the research techniques described in this book. The Marketing Science Institute has been formed in the last few years to pursue basic and applied studies toward the establishment of science in marketing. It is significant that its support funds have been provided by industrial sponsors, including advertising agencies and business consulting firms.

Concomitant with increased emphasis on research, university course materials are reflecting the need to train students in the newer decision-making tools. It is not uncommon now to have required courses in the calculus, matrix algebra, probability theory, and computer programming for all incoming students at the graduate level. Moreover, not only marketing but other functional areas of business — finance, accounting, production management — are reflecting, by research and teaching, a greater emphasis on quantitative techniques.

This trend has not been restricted to business schools, however. Howard [106] reports that General Electric has stored in its central computer a sophisticated investment model adapted to decision making under uncertainty.

An executive with an investment problem, for example, the decision of whether to initiate a new product, sits down at the console's typewriter keyboard and punches the number which pulls the capital budgeting program from storage in the central computer at Phoenix, Arizona. Then, as a result of signals from the central computer, the typewriter begins to type out the questions the executive must answer to obtain the rate of return on his proposed investment. The questions asked of him are, for example, "What is your planning horizon?" "What volume of sales do you expect from your new product during each year of that planning horizon?", etc. Within ten or fifteen minutes from the time the executive sat down at the console he can have fed in his answers and received the rate of return figure he is seeking. [107]

In view of Howard's remarks, it is not surprising that many companies are making concerted efforts to provide their personnel with "in-house" lectures and courses as part of a continued training program to update their methodological skills.

This proliferation of methodological innovations, of course, has not been an unmixed blessing for either universities or industrial firms. Business schools have had to train some of their own faculty members in the newer tools. Curricula have gone through rather drastic and sometimes traumatic changes. Business firms have had trouble seeking and retaining competent people who are versed in the new technology. As in any period of change, serious errors have occurred in the zeal to "keep up with the latest" in methodology.

Despite the inevitable misapplication of techniques and overselling (with the consequent failure to live up to expectations), the fact remains that quantitative and behavioral science are here to stay. Nor does their application appear to be restricted to the industrial giants. With such opportunities as "shared-time" arrangements, even smaller firms can avail themselves of high-investment equipment such as computing facilities.

Growing involvement of the line manager in marketing research

In Chapter 1 we first suggested that some of the newer decision tools require managerial participation with the researcher and that the fact-gathering role of marketing research is declining in favor of viewing the role of research as a means for reducing the costs of uncertainty in managerial decision making.

In our judgment the changes that are taking place in educational institutions will affect the line executive as well as the staff specialist. The manager can ill afford to insulate himself from these developments. Rather than making his role more passive, the use of behavioral and management science should increase his importance. The staff specialist is usually not privy to the many sources of information — structured or not — that the marketing manager has at his disposal. Moreover, it is the marketing manager who is usually in the best position to comment critically on the realism of the model's assumption structure. As mentioned earlier, we believe that the "dialogue process" between manager and researcher will increase rather than decrease in importance as research methodology is applied to higher-level problems.

The research generalist

In line with our preceding comments we would add, in a more speculative vein, that future years may see the emergence of the research generalist whose job will be to perform many of the communication and evaluative chores between line executive and staff personnel who are becoming increasingly specialized and technical. This hunch is not as fanciful as it may seem at first.

With the proliferation of specialties and their accompanying jargon, it is becoming increasingly difficult for even technicians to communicate with each other. The appearance of new journal after journal is witness to the fact that the disciplines themselves are becoming increasingly fragmented. A few years ago a marketing academician interested in quantitative techniques could maintain a fairly good grasp of the entire field. Today we have quantitative "subspecialists" in decision theory, Markov processes, multivariate analysis, and so on. There is good reason to believe that marketing researchers in business will not remain immune to this growing trend toward specialization.

A research generalist presumably would be a person who can converse with *both* managers and researchers. Although he will have technical training and be familiar with the jargon of the specialist, his value system would be compatible with management. It would be his responsibility to evaluate the research in terms of *practical and actionable implications*. The authors of this book already know of a few companies who have started active development of such research generalists.

The establishment of this function is, of course, not to imply that the marketing executive can abdicate his responsibility for keeping up with the changes taking place in research methodology. But practical limitations on his time and the speed with which developments in this area are occurring should make the function of the research generalist a useful aid to both manager and researcher.

The Road Ahead

We have tried to convey in this short book some impression of the changes which have taken place and are continuing to occur in the strategy and tactics of marketing research. We hope we have transmitted some of the excitement of these new developments without glossing over the limitations of current concepts and techniques.

Our presentation has been nontechnical and the scope of our coverage has limited the detail in which the new methodology is treated. We do hope, however, that there has been enough discussed here to stimulate the reader — line manager or staff man —

to make his own inquiry into, and evaluation of, these developments. (Chapter 6 has been prepared to assist the reader in this endeavor.)

In closing we know of no better way to evaluate the worth of these techniques (and their users) than has already been so succinctly expressed by Ackoff and Rivett [6]:

He (the researcher) must be willing to be judged by the manager in exactly the same way the manager has to be judged, namely, on the basis of the performance of his recommendations when they are put into operation.

6 Further Reading

In the first five chapters of this book we have tried to give the reader some idea of the developments that are taking place in marketing research concept and technique. Naturally space considerations have limited the detail in which these developments could be discussed. In this concluding chapter we present a brief tour of the literature. In addition, we hope the reader will take time to examine some of the many references cited in the chapters.

Because technical backgrounds and interests will surely vary, we have included references that range in mathematical complexity from nontechnical expositions to fairly sophisticated research monographs.

Journals

Today's marketing researcher is obliged to cover an increasingly varied group of journals for techniques and models developed by related disciplines.

The primary group of journals for the professional marketing researcher is the following:

Journal of Marketing (Quarterly Publication of the American Marketing Association, 230 North Michigan Avenue, Chicago, Ill.)

Journal of Marketing Research (Quarterly Publication of the American Marketing Association, 230 North Michigan Avenue, Chicago, Ill.)

Journal of Advertising Research (Quarterly Publication of the Advertising Research Foundation, 3 East 54th Street, New York, N. Y.)

The first of these three journals is nontechnical and contains articles of interest to both line and staff marketers. The last two publications are considerably more technical but will keep the reader apprised of current developments in technique. All three journals carry reviews of current books in marketing, and the *Journal of Marketing* presents abstracts of most of the current literature on marketing which appears in other journals.

In addition to these journals, the marketing staff man may at times wish to peruse other journals which sometimes discuss material of interest to the professional. Illustrations of this type of journal are the following:

> *Public Opinion Quarterly* (Quarterly Publication of the American Association for Public Opinion Research, P. O. Box 231, Princeton, N. J.)
>
> *The American Behavioral Scientist* (Monthly Publication, except July and August, 80 East 11th Street, New York, N. Y.)
>
> *Behavioral Science* (Bi-monthly Publication of the Mental Health Research Institute, The University of Michigan and of The Institute of Management Sciences. Published at Mt. Royal and Guilford Avenues, Baltimore, Md.)
>
> *Multivariate Behavioral Research* (Quarterly Publication of Texas Christian University, Fort Worth, Texas.)
>
> *Operations Research* (Bi-monthly Publication of the Operations Research Society of America. Published at Mount Royal and Guilford Avenues, Baltimore, Md.)
>
> *Management Science* (Monthly Publication of the Institute of Management Sciences. Published at Mount Royal and Guilford Avenues, Baltimore, Md.)

The first two publications present fairly nontechnical discussions of recent techniques in the social sciences of interest to the marketing researcher. The second two publications are more technically oriented and are prepared for the professional working in these fields. The last two journals frequently contain discussions of mathematical models of interest to the quantitatively oriented marketing researcher.

In addition to the foregoing sources, articles of interest to the marketing researcher appear in such "general" business publications as the *Harvard Business Review, Journal of Business, Business Horizons,* and *California Management Review.* Other sources of current materials may be found in various foreign publications, such as *Commentary, Operational Research Quarterly, Applied Statistics* (English), and *Metro* (French). The Proceedings of the American Marketing Association provides current materials of interest to both line and staff marketers.

Marketing Research Texts

There are a number of fairly general accounts of marketing research with which the practitioner should have some familiarity. Among these are the following:

- Boyd, H. W., Jr., and R. Westfall, *Marketing Research: Texts and Cases* (Homewood, Ill.: Richard D. Irwin, 1964).
- Ferber, R., D. F. Blankertz, and S. Hollander, Jr., *Marketing Research* (New York: The Ronald Press Co., 1964).
- Schreier, F. T., *Modern Marketing Research: A Behavioral Approach* (Belmont, Cal.: Wadsworth Publishing Co., 1963).
- Green, P. E., and D. S. Tull, *Research for Marketing Decisions* (Englewood Cliffs, N. J.: Prentice-Hall, Inc., 1966).

The first two books are comprehensive texts in the general area of marketing research. The Schreier book presents some interesting material dealing with behavioral science applications to marketing research at a nontechnical level. The Green and Tull book presents a more detailed (and more technical) discussion of many of the concepts and techniques discussed in this volume.

Specialized Materials for the Marketing Researcher

For the marketing research professional who desires to peruse more specialized literature dealing with behavioral science, statistical techniques, and mathematical models, we would recommend the following:

- Frank, R. E., A. A. Kuehn, and W. F. Massy, *Quantitative Techniques in Marketing* (Homewood, Ill.: Richard D. Irwin, Inc., 1963).
- Selltiz, C., et al., *Research Methods in Social Relations* (New York: Holt, Rinehart and Winston, 1964).
- Kerlinger, F. N., *Foundations of Behavioral Research* (New York: Holt, Rinehart and Winston, 1964).

Torgerson, W. S., *Theory and Methods of Scaling* (New York: John Wiley and Sons, 1960).

- Cooley, W. W., and P. R. Lohnes, *Multivariate Procedures for the Behavioral Sciences* (New York: John Wiley and Sons, 1962).
- Day, R. L., *Marketing Models: Quantitative and Behavioral* (Scranton, Pa.: International Textbook Co., 1964).

Bass, F., et al. (eds.), *Mathematical Models and Methods of Marketing* (Homewood, Ill.: Richard D. Irwin, 1961).

Alderson, W., and P. E. Green, *Planning and Problem Solving in Marketing* (Homewood, Ill.: Richard D. Irwin, 1964).

Churchman, C. W., R. L. Ackoff, and E. L. Arnoff, *Introduction to Operations Research* (New York: John Wiley and Sons, 1957).

- Ackoff, R. L., *Scientific Method: Optimizing Applied Research Decisions* (New York: John Wiley and Sons, 1962).

The book by Frank, Kuehn, and Massy provides the reader with an exposition of such techniques as experimental design, multivariate analysis and simulation as well as a set of readings dealing with various aspects of measurement, inference, and descriptive model building in marketing. The books by Selltiz et al. and Kerlinger, although addressed to behavioral science research procedures, contain much material which is relevant to the design, conduct, and analysis of marketing research investigations. The Torgerson and Cooley and Lohnes books deal, respectively, with psychological scaling and multivariate analysis. Although technically oriented, they are basic introductions to these increasingly important classes of techniques.

The books by Day and Bass et al. are excellent reading books. The first includes both quantitative and behavioral models. The second is restricted to prescriptive models, but it contains excellent nontechnical introductions to each article and appendices for the reader interested in the mathematical aspects of the models. The Alderson and Green book is a fairly nontechnical discussion of various models and statistical techniques of interest to the marketing planner.

The book by Churchman, Ackoff, and Arnoff, although devoted to operations research procedures, is relevant for model-building procedures in marketing. Finally, the Ackoff book, which deals with experimental inquiry and the philosophy of science, contains much relevant material for the serious practitioner of marketing research.

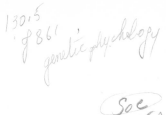

References

[1] Ackoff, R. L., *Scientific Method: Optimizing Applied Research Decisions* (New York: John Wiley and Sons, 1962), p. 178.

[2] *Ibid.*, Chapter 11, pp. 342–378.

[3] Ackoff, R. L., "Allocation of Sales Effort," *Proceedings of the Conference on What is Operations Research Accomplishing in Industry?,* Case Institute of Technology, April 1955, pp. 23–30.

[4] Ackoff, R. L., "Rounding out the Management Sciences," *Columbia Journal of World Business,* Vol. 1 (Winter 1966), pp. 33–36.

[5] Ackoff, R. L., and P. Rivett, *A Manager's Guide to Operations Research* (New York: John Wiley and Sons, 1964).

[6] *Ibid.*, p. 98.

[7] Alderson, W., and P. E. Green, *Planning and Problem Solving in Marketing* (Homewood, Ill.: Richard D. Irwin, 1964), p. 229.

[8] *Ibid.*, p. 274.

[9] Anderson, R. L., and T. A. Bancroft, *Statistical Theory in Research* (New York: McGraw-Hill Book Co., 1952).

[10] Anderson, T. W., *Introduction to Multivariate Statistical Analysis,* (New York: John Wiley and Sons, 1958).

[11] Balderston, F. E., "Communication Networks in Intermediate Markets," *Management Science,* Vol. 4 (January 1958), pp. 156–171.

[12] Balderston, F. E., and A. C. Hoggatt, "Simulating Market Processes," in *Marketing Models: Quantitative and Behavioral,* R. L. Day (ed.) (Scranton, Pa.: International Textbook Co., 1964), pp. 156–171.

[13] Banks, A. S., and P. M. Gregg, "Grouping Political Systems: Q-Factor Analysis of a Cross-Policy Survey," *The American Behavioral Scientist,* Vol. 9 (November 1965), pp. 3–6.

[14] Banks, Seymour, *Experimentation in Marketing* (New York: McGraw-Hill Book Co., 1965).

[15] *Ibid.*, pp. 128–134.

[16] Banks, S., "Designing Marketing Research to Increase Validity," *Journal of Marketing,* Vol. 28 (October 1964), pp. 32–40.

[17] Banks, S., "The Relationship Between Preference and Purchase of Brands," *Journal of Marketing,* Vol. 15 (October 1950), pp. 145–57.

[18] Bass, F. M., "Marketing Research Expenditures: A Decision Model," *Journal of Business,* Vol. 36 (January 1963), pp. 77–90.

[19] Becknell, James, Jr., and Robert W. McIssac, "Test Marketing Cookware Coated with Teflon," *Journal of Advertising Research,* Vol. 5 (September 1963).

[20] Bellman, R. E., *Dynamic Programming* (Princeton, N.J.: Princeton University Press, 1962).

[21] Benson, P. H., "A Short Method for Estimating a Distribution of Consumer Preferences," *Journal of Applied Psychology,* Vol. 46, No. 5 (1962), pp. 307–313.

[22] Bernstein, A., "Computer Simulation of Media Exposures," *Sixth Meeting of the Advertising Research Foundation Operations Discussion Group,* New York (1961).

[23] Britt, S. H., and H. W. Boyd, Jr., "Making Marketing Research More Effective by Using the Administrative Process," *Journal of Marketing Research,* Vol. 2 (February 1965), pp. 13–19.

[24] Brown, D. B., and M. R. Warshaw, "Media Selection by Linear Programming," *Journal of Marketing Research,* Vol. 2 (February 1965), pp. 83–88.

[25] Brown, George H., "Measuring the Sales Effectiveness of Alternative Media," *Seventh Annual Conference of the Advertising Research Foundation* (October 1961).

[26] Brown, Sidney E., *Increasing Broiler Sales through Offering an Additional Cut and Recipe Materials,* U. S. Department of Agriculture, Economic Research Service No. 127 (May 1963).

[27] Buhler, Ronald, *P-Stat: A System of Statistical Programs for the 7090/94, Princeton University* (February 1964).

[28] *Business Week,* "Scouting the Trail for Marketers," Special Report (April 18, 1964).

[29] Buzzell, R. D., *Mathematical Models and Marketing Management* (Boston: Graduate School of Business Administration, Harvard University, 1964).

[30] Buzzell, R. D., and C. C. Slater, "Decision Theory and Marketing Management," *Journal of Marketing,* Vol. 26 (July 1962), pp. 7–16.

[31] Cardoza, R. N., "An Experimental Study of Consumer Effort, Expectation and Satisfaction," *Journal of Marketing Research,* Vol. 2 (August 1965), pp. 244–249.

[32] Charnes, A., and W. W. Cooper, "The Stepping Stone Method of Explaining Linear Programming Calculations in Transport Problems," *Management Science,* Vol. 1 (October 1954), pp. 49–69.

[33] Chernoff, H., and L. E. Moses, *Elementary Decision Theory* (New York: John Wiley and Sons, 1959).

[34] Claycamp, Henry J., "Characteristics of Owners of Thrift Deposits in Commercial Banks and Savings and Loan Associations," *Journal of Marketing Research,* Vol. 2 (May 1965), pp. 163–170.

[35] Clevenger, T., G. A. Lazier, and M. L. Clark, "Measurement of Corporate Images by Semantic Differential," *Journal of Marketing Research,* Vol. 2 (February 1965), pp. 80–82.

[36] Cochran, W. G., and Gertrude M. Cox, *Experimental Designs* (New York: John Wiley and Sons, 1957).

[37] *Ibid.,* pp. 82–91.

[38] Coleman, J., H. Menzel, and E. Katz, "Social Processes in Physicians' Adoption of a New Drug," reprinted in *Quantitative Techniques in Marketing Analysis*, R. E. Frank, A. A. Kuehn, and W. F. Massy (eds.) (Homewood, Ill.: Richard D. Irwin, 1962), pp. 239–264.

[39] Colley, R. H. (ed.), *Defining Advertising Goals for Measured Advertising Results* (New York: Association of National Advertisers, 1961).

[40] "Color Study Checks Sales in Stores," *Editor and Publisher* (June 13, 1959).

[41] Cook, W., and M. H. Halbert, "Rate Analysis in a Public Utility," in *Proceedings of the Conference on Case Studies in Operations Research*, Case Institute of Technology (February 1965), pp. 48–52.

[42] Cooley, W. W., and Paul R. Lohnes, *Multivariate Procedures for the Behavioral Sciences* (New York: John Wiley and Sons, 1962).

[43] *Ibid.*, pp. 35–37.

[44] Cox, D. R., *Planning of Experiments* (New York: John Wiley and Sons, 1958).

[45] *Ibid.*, pp. 48–69.

[46] Cox, D. F., and S. Rich, "Perceived Risk and Consumer Decision Making," *Journal of Marketing Research*, Vol. 1 (November 1964), pp. 32–39.

[47] Crane, E., *Marketing Communications* (New York: John Wiley and Sons, 1965), p. 10.

[48] Crespi, L., "Use of a Scaling Technique in Surveys," *Journal of Marketing*, Vol. 25 (July 1961), pp. 69–72.

[49] Christensen, B. M., and J. R. Greene, "Planning, Scheduling and Controlling the Launching of a New Product Via CPM," in *Marketing and the Computer*, W. Alderson and S. J. Shapiro (eds.) (Englewood Cliffs, N. J.: Prentice-Hall, 1963), pp. 178–200.

[50] Christenson, C., *Strategic Aspects of Competitive Bidding for Corporate Securities* (Boston: Division of Research, Graduate School of Business Administration, Harvard University, 1965).

[51] Cronbach, L., and G. C. Gleser, "Assessing Similarity Between Profiles," *The Psychological Bulletin*, Vol. 50, No. 6, pp. 456–473.

[52] Day, R. L., "Systematic Paired Comparisons in Preference Analysis," *Journal of Marketing Research*, Vol. 2 (November 1965), pp. 406–412.

[53] DeVoe, J. K., "Plans, Profits and the Marketing Program," *Proceedings of 48th National Conference of the American Marketing Association*, New York (June 1965), pp. 473–488.

[54] Dichter, E., "Toward an Understanding of Human Behavior," in *Motivation and Market Behavior*, R. Ferber and H. Wales (eds.) (Homewood, Ill.: Richard D. Irwin, 1958).

[55] Dixon, W. J., *BMD: Biomedial Computer Programs, Health Science Computing Facility*, Department of Preventive Medicine and Public Health, School of Medicine, University of California, Los Angeles (January 1, 1964).

[56] Dixon, W. J., and F. J. Massey, *Introduction to Statistical Analysis* (New York: McGraw-Hill Book Co., 1957).

[57] Domenick, B. A., *Merchandising McIntosh Apples Under Controlled Conditions — Customer Reaction and Effect on Sales* (Unpublished Ph.D. Dissertation, Cornell University, 1952).

[58] Dorfman, R., and P. O. Steiner, "Optimal Advertising and Optimal Quality," *The American Economic Review,* Vol. 44 (December 1954), pp. 826–36.

[59] Draper, J. E., and L. H. Nolin, "A Markov Analysis of Brand Preference," *Journal of Advertising Research,* Vol. 4 (September 1964), pp. 33–38.

[60] Dunlop, J. W., "The Effect of Color in Direct Mail Advertising," *Journal of Applied Psychology,* Vol. 34 (1950), pp. 280–283.

[61] Eastlack, J. L., "Consumer Flavor Preference Factors in Food Product Design," *Journal of Marketing Research,* Vol. 1 (February 1964), pp. 38–42.

[62] Edwards, W., and L. D. Phillips, "Man as a Transducer for Probabilities in Bayesian Command and Control Systems," in *Human Judgments and Optimality,* M. W. Shelley and G. L. Bryan (eds.) (New York: John Wiley and Sons, 1964), pp. 360–401.

[63] Ehrenberg, A. S. C., "An Appraisal of Markov Brand-Switching Models," *Journal of Marketing Research,* Vol. 2 (November 1965), pp. 347–362.

[64] Engel, J. F., and M. R. Warshaw, "Allocating Advertising Dollars by Linear Programming," *Journal of Advertising Research,* Vol. 4 (September 1964), pp. 42–48.

[65] Evans, F. B., "Psychological and Objective Factors in the Prediction of Brand Choice, Ford versus Chevrolet," *Journal of Business,* Vol. 32 (October 1959), pp. 340–369.

[66] Ezekiel, M., and K. A. Fox, *Methods of Correlation and Regression Analysis* (New York: John Wiley and Sons, 1959).

[67] Farley, J. V., "Why Does Brand Loyalty Vary Over Products?," *Journal of Marketing Research,* Vol. 1 (November 1964), pp. 9–14.

[68] Farley, J. V., "An Optimal Plan for Salesmen's Compensation," *Journal of Marketing Research,* Vol. 1 (May 1964), pp. 39–43.

[69] Federer, W. T., *Experimental Design* (New York: The Macmillan Co., 1955).

[70] *Ibid.,* pp. 482–522.

[71] Forrester, J. W., "Advertising: A Problem in Industrial Dynamics," *Harvard Business Review,* Vol. 37 (March–April 1959), pp. 100–110.

[72] Frank, R. E., "Brand Choice as a Probability Process," *Journal of Business,* Vol. 35 (January 1962), pp. 43–56.

[73] Frank, R. E., and H. W. Boyd, Jr., "Are Private Brand-Prone Grocery Customers Really Different?" *Journal of Advertising Research,* Vol. 5 (December 1965), pp. 27–35.

[74] *Ibid.,* pp. 31–32.

[75] Frank, R. E., and W. F. Massy, "Market Segmentation and the Effectiveness of a Brand's Price and Dealing Policies," *Journal of Business,* Vol. 38 (April 1965), pp. 182–200.

[76] Frank, R. E., W. F. Massy, and D. G. Morrison, "The Determinants of Innovative Behavior with Respect to a Branded, Frequently Purchased Food Product," *Proceedings of the American Marketing Association,* December 1964, pp. 312–323.

[77] Friedman, L., "A Competitive Bidding Strategy," *Journal of the Operations Research Society of America,* Vol. 4 (February 1956), pp. 104–112.

[78] Green, P. E., "Bayesian Statistics and Product Decisions," *Business Horizons,* Vol. 5 (Fall 1962), pp. 101–109.

[79] Green, P. E., "Bayesian Decision Theory in Advertising," *Journal of Advertising Research,* Vol. 2 (December 1962), pp. 33–41.

[80] Green, P. E., "Decision Theory and Chemical Marketing," *Industrial and Engineering Chemistry,* Vol. 54 (September 1962), pp. 30–34.

[81] Green, P. E., "Bayesian Decision Theory in Pricing Strategy," *Journal of Marketing,* Vol. 27 (January 1963), pp. 5–14.

[82] Green, P. E., "Risk Attitudes and Chemical Investment Decisions," *Chemical Engineering Progress,* Vol. 39 (January 1963), pp. 35–40.

[83] Green, P. E., "Marketing Theory and the Literature of the Management Sciences," in *The Meaning and Sources of Marketing Theory,* by M. H. Halbert (New York: McGraw-Hill Book Co., 1965), p. 128.

[84] *Ibid.,* p. 136.

[85] Green, P. E., R. E. Frank, and P. J. Robinson, "Cluster Analysis in Test Market Selection," Mimeographed, May 1966.

[86] Green, P. E., M. H. Halbert, and P. J. Robinson, "Canonical Analysis: An Exposition and Illustrative Application," *Journal of Marketing Research,* Vol. 3 (February 1966), pp. 32–39.

[87] Green, P. E., M. H. Halbert, and P. J. Robinson, "Experimental Gaming in Consumer Brand Choice Behavior," *The Business Quarterly,* Vol. 30 (Fall 1965), pp. 49–56.

[88] Green, P. E., W. S. Peters, and P. J. Robinson, "A Behavioral Experiment in Decision-Making under Uncertainty," *Journal of Purchasing,* Vol. 2 (February 1966), pp. 18–31.

[89] Green, P. E., and D. S. Tull, *Research for Marketing Decisions* (Englewood Cliffs, N.J.: Prentice-Hall, 1966), Chapter 1.

[90] *Ibid.,* p. 411.

[91] *Ibid.,* p. 433.

[92] Gross, I., "How Many Ads Does it Pay to Pretest?" *Tenth Meeting of the Advertising Research Foundation Operations Research Discussion Group,* New York, March 10, 1964, pp. 1–18.

[93] Grubb, Violet D., H. Smith, M. Wischkaempfer, and N. Havas, "Effectiveness of Selected Canned Food Displays in Supermarkets," U. S. Department of Agriculture, *Marketing Research Report NA 371,* November 1959.

[94] Guttman, L., "Measuring the True State of Opinion," in *Motivation and Market Behavior,* R. Ferber and H. Wales (eds.) (Homewood, Ill.: Richard D. Irwin, 1958).

[95] Hamilton, O. W., "On Determining an Optimum Guarantee Policy,"

Proceedings of the Conference on Operations Research in Marketing, Case Institute of Technology, January 1953, pp. 19–24.

[96] Harary, F., and B. Lipstein, "The Dynamics of Brand Loyalty: A Markovian Approach," *Operations Research,* Vol. 10 (February 1962), pp. 19–40.

[97] Harper, R., "Factor Analysis as a Technique for Examining Complex Data on Foodstuffs," *Applied Statistics,* Vol. 5 (March 1956), pp. 32–48.

[98] Harris, D., "Predicting Consumer Reaction to Product Designs," *Journal of Advertising Research,* Vol. 4 (June 1964), pp. 34–37.

[99] Harvey, J., "What Makes a Best Seller?" in *Motivation and Market Behavior,* R. Ferber and H. G. Wales (eds.) (Homewood, Ill.: Richard D. Irwin, 1958), pp. 361–381.

[100] Henderson, P. L., J. F. Hind, and S. E. Brown, *Promotional Programs for Lamb and Their Effects on Sales,* U. S. Department of Agriculture, Market Research Report No. 522, January 1962.

[101] Henderson, P. L., J. F. Hind, and S. E. Brown, "Sales Effect of Two Campaign Themes," *Journal of Advertising Research,* Vol. 1 (December 1961), pp. 2–11.

[102] *Ibid.,* pp. 6–9.

[103] Hertz, D. B., "Risk Analysis in Capital Investment," *Harvard Business Review,* Vol. 42 (January–February 1964), pp. 95–106.

[104] Holloway, R. J., and T. White, "Advancing the Experimental Method in Marketing," *Journal of Marketing Research,* Vol. 7 (February 1964), pp. 25–29.

[105] Hoofnagle, W. S., "Experimental Designs in Measuring the Effectiveness of Promotion," *Journal of Marketing Research,* Vol. 2 (May 1965), p. 157.

[106] Howard, J. A., "Marketing Education 1965," *Proceedings of the Fall Conference of the American Marketing Association,* Washington, D. C. (September 1965), pp. 745–752.

[107] *Ibid.,* p. 746.

[108] Howard, R. A., "Stochastic Process Models of Consumer Behavior," *Journal of Advertising Research,* Vol. 3 (September 1963), pp. 35–42.

[109] Johnston, J., *Econometric Methods* (New York: McGraw-Hill Book Co., 1963).

[110] Kelley, W. T., "Marketing Intelligence for Top Management," *Journal of Marketing,* Vol. 29 (October 1965), pp. 19–24.

[111] Kempthorne, O., *The Design and Analysis of Experiments* (New York: John Wiley and Sons, Inc., 1952).

[112] Kendall, M. G., *A Course in Multivariate Statistics* (London: Charles Griffin and Co., 1951).

[113] *Ibid.,* pp. 68–85.

[114] King, W. R., "Marketing Expansion — A Statistical Analysis," *Management Science,* Vol. 9 (July 1963), pp. 563–573.

[115] Kotler, P., "Behavioral Models for Analyzing Buyers," *Journal of Marketing,* Vol. 29 (October 1965), pp. 37–45.

[116] Kotler, P., "Toward an Explicit Model for Media Selection," *Journal of Advertising Research*, Vol. 4 (March 1964), pp. 34–41.

[117] Kotler, P., "The Use of Mathematical Models in Marketing," *Journal of Marketing*, Vol. 27 (October 1963), pp. 31–41.

[118] *Ibid.*, pp. 40–41.

[119] Krantz, F. A., "An Analysis of Some Factors that Might Influence the Volume of Sales of Small, Medium and Large Potatoes in a Controlled Experiment of Consumer Preferences," *Proceedings of the American Society for Horticultural Science*, Vol. 55 (1950), pp. 427–434.

[120] Kuehn, A. A., "Consumer Brand Choice as a Learning Process," *Journal of Advertising Research*, Vol. 2 (December 1962), pp. 10–17.

[121] Kuehn, A. A., and R. L. Day, "Strategy of Product Quality," *Harvard Business Review*, Vol. 40 (November–December 1962), pp. 100–110.

[122] Kuehn, A. A., and M. S. Hamburger, "A Heuristic Program for Locating Warehouses," *Management Science*, Vol. 9 (July 1963), pp. 643–666.

[123] Lakshmanan, T. R., and W. G. Hansen, "A Retail Market Potential Model," *Journal of the American Institute of Planners*, Vol. 31 (May 1965), pp. 134–143.

[124] Learner, D. B., "DEMON New Product Planning: A Case History," *Proceedings of 48th National Conference of American Marketing Association*, New York, June 1965, pp. 489–508.

[125] Levy, S. S., "Social Class and Consumer Behavior," in *On Knowing the Consumer*, J. W. Newman (ed.) (New York: John Wiley and Sons, 1966), pp. 146–160.

[126] Lipstein, B., "Prospects for the Managerial Sciences in Advertising," *Paper presented at the American Meeting of the Institute of Management Sciences*, Dallas, Texas, February 1966.

[127] Little, J. D. C., "A Model of Adaptive Control of Promotional Spending," Sloan School of Industrial Management, Massachusetts Institute of Technology, Cambridge, Mass., 1965.

[128] Maffei, R. B., "Brand Preferences and Simple Markov Processes," *Operations Research*, Vol. 8 (March 1960), pp. 210–18.

[129] Magee, J. F., "How to Use Decision Trees in Capital Investment," *Harvard Business Review*, Vol. 42 (September–October 1964), pp. 79–96.

[130] Magee, J. F., "The Effect of Promotional Effort on Sales," *Journal of the Operations Research Society*, Vol. 1 (February 1953), pp. 64–74.

[131] Magee, J. F., "The Logistics of Distribution," *Harvard Business Review*, Vol. 38 (July–August 1960), pp. 89–101.

[132] *Market Facts, Inc.*, "Product Evaluation: An Examination of Research Procedures," March 1962, p. 30.

[133] Marquardt, R., J. Makens, and H. Larzelere, "Measuring the Utility Added by Branding and Grading," *Journal of Marketing Research*, Vol. 2 (February 1965), pp. 45–50.

[134] Massy, W. F., "Discriminant Analysis of Audience Characteristics," *Journal of Advertising Research*, Vol. 5 (March 1965), pp. 39–48.

[135] *Ibid.,* pp. 39–48.

[136] Massy, W. F., "Applying Factor Analysis to a Specific Marketing Problem," *Proceedings of the American Marketing Association* (December 1963), pp. 291–307.

[137] Miller, G. A., "The Magical Number Seven, Plus or Minus Two: Some Limits on our Capacity for Processing Information," *Psychological Review,* Vol. 63 (1956), pp. 81–97.

[138] Mindak, W. A., "Fitting the Semantic Differential to the Marketing Problem," *Journal of Marketing,* Vol. 25 (April 1961), pp. 28–33.

[139] Nordin, J. A., "Spatial Allocation of Selling Expense," *Journal of Marketing,* Vol. 7 (January 1943), pp. 210–19.

[140] O'Meara, Jr., J. T., "Selecting Profitable Products," *Harvard Business Review,* Vol. 39 (January–February 1961), pp. 83–89.

[141] Osgood, C. E., G. J. Suci, and P. H. Tannenbaum, *The Measurement of Meaning* (Urbana, Ill.: University of Illinois Press, 1957).

[142] Pessemier, E. A., "An Experimental Method of Estimating Demand," *Journal of Business,* Vol. 33 (October 1960), pp. 373–383.

[143] Prager, W., "On Warehousing Problems," *Operations Research,* Vol. 5 (August 1957), pp. 504–512.

[144] Rao, C. R., *Advanced Statistical Methods in Biometric Research* (New York: John Wiley and Sons, Inc., 1952).

[145] Ratoosh, P., "Experimental Studies of Implementation," *Working Paper 117,* Center for Research in Management Science, University of California, Berkeley, Cal. (May 1965).

[146] Richards, E. A., "A Commercial Application of Guttman Scaling Techniques," *Journal of Marketing,* Vol. 22 (October 1957), pp. 166–173.

[147] Roberts, H. V., "The New Business Statistics," *Journal of Business,* Vol. 33 (January 1960), pp. 21–30.

[148] Roberts, H. V., "Bayesian Statistics in Marketing," *Journal of Marketing,* Vol. 27 (January 1963), pp. 1–4.

[149] Robinson, P. J., and D. Luck, *Promotional Decision Making: Practice and Theory* (New York: McGraw-Hill Book Co., 1964), p. 221.

[150] Schlaifer, R., *Probability and Statistics for Business Decisions* (New York: McGraw-Hill Book Co., 1959).

[151] Schwerin Research Corp., "Why TV Commercials Succeed," in R. E. Frank, A. A. Kuehn, and W. F. Massy, *Quantitative Techniques in Marketing Analysis* (Homewood, Ill.: Richard D. Irwin, 1962), pp. 166–176.

[152] Scriven, L. E., "Rationality and Irrationality in Motivation Research," in *Motivation and Market Behavior,* R. Ferber and H. Wales (eds.) (Homewood, Ill.: Richard D. Irwin, Inc., 1958), pp. 64–72.

[153] Selltiz, C., M. Jahoda, M. Deutsch, and S. W. Cook, *Research Methods in Social Relations* (New York: Holt, Rinehart and Winston, 1964).

[154] Shaw, S. J., "Behavioral Science Offers Fresh Insights on New Product Acceptance," *Journal of Marketing,* Vol. 29 (January 1965), pp. 9–13.

[155] Simon, H. A., and A. Newell, "Heuristic Problem Solving," *Operations Research,* Vol. 6 (January 1958), p. 3.

[156] Simon, L. S., "Measuring the Market Impact of Technical Service," *Journal of Marketing Research,* Vol. 2 (February 1965), pp. 32–39.

[157] Simulmatics Corporation, "The Simulmatics Media-Mix: Technical Description," New York, October 1962.

[158] Smith, H. M., W. Clement, and W. S. Hoofnagle, "Merchandising Natural Cheddar Cheese in Retail Food Stores," U. S. Department of Agriculture, *Market Research Report No. 115,* April 1956.

[159] Smith, H. M., and R. Frye, "How Color of Red Delicious Apples Affects Their Sales, U. S. Department of Agriculture, *Market Research Report No. 618,* February 1964.

[160] Snedecor, G. W., *Statistical Methods* (Ames, Iowa: Iowa State College Press, 1956).

[161] Spector, A. J., "Basic Dimensions of Corporate Image," *Journal of Marketing,* Vol. 23 (October 1961), pp. 47–51.

[162] Starbuck, W. H., and F. M. Bass, "An Experimental Study of Risk-Taking and the Value of Information in a New Product Context," *Institute Paper 117,* Herman C. Krannert Graduate School of Industrial Administration, Purdue University, 1964.

[163] Steele, H. L., "On the Validity of Projective Questions," *Journal of Marketing Research,* Vol. 1 (August 1964), pp. 46–49.

[164] Stefflre, V., "Simulation of People's Behavior toward New Objects and Events," *The American Behavioral Scientist,* Vol. 8 (May 1965), pp. 12–15.

[165] Stephenson, W., *The Study of Behavior* (Chicago: University of Chicago Press, 1953).

[166] Stevens, S. S., "Mathematics, Measurement and Psychophysics," in *Handbook of Experimental Psychology,* S. S. Stevens (ed.) (New York: John Wiley and Sons, 1962).

[167] Stewart, C. T., "Migration as a Function of Population and Distance," *American Sociological Review,* Vol. 25 (June 1960), pp. 347–56.

[168] Stone, P. J., D. C. Dunphy, and A. Bernstein, "Content Analysis Applications at Simulmatics," *The American Behavioral Scientist,* Vol. 8 (May 1965), pp. 16–18.

[169] Styan, G. P. H., and H. Smith, Jr., "Markov Chains Applied to Marketing," *Journal of Marketing Research,* Vol. 1 (February 1964), pp. 50–55.

[170] Thurstone, L. L., *The Measurement of Values* (Chicago: University of Chicago Press, 1959).

[171] *Ibid.,* pp. 195–210.

[172] Torgerson, W. S., *Theory and Methods of Scaling* (New York: John Wiley and Sons, 1960).

[173] Tucker, W. T., "The Development of Brand Loyalty," *Journal of Marketing Research,* Vol. 1 (August 1964), pp. 32–35.

[174] Twedt, D., "A Multiple Factor Analysis of Advertising Readership," *Journal of Applied Psychology,* Vol. 1 (November 1964), pp. 9–14.

[175] Varnum, E. C., "Sales Office Potential," *Proceedings of the Confer-*

ence on Operations Research in Marketing, Case Institute of Technology, January 1953, pp. 16–18.

[176] Vicary, J. M., "How Psychiatric Methods Can Be Applied to Market Research," in *Motivation and Market Behavior,* R. Ferber and H. Wales (eds.) (Homewood, Ill.: Richard D. Irwin, Inc., 1958), pp. 31–36.

[177] Vidale, M. L., and H. B. Wolfe, "An Operations Research Study of Sales Response to Advertising," *Operations Research,* Vol. 5 (June 1957), pp. 370–381.

[178] von Neumann, J., and O. Morgenstern, *Theory of Games and Economic Behavior* (Princeton, N.J.: Princeton University Press, 1953).

[179] Watson, J. B., and W. McDougall, *The Battle of Behaviorism* (New York: W. W. Norton and Co., 1929).

[180] Webster, F. E., Jr., "Modeling the Industrial Buying Process," *Journal of Marketing Research,* Vol. 2 (November 1965), pp. 370–376.

[181] Weinberg, R. S., "Management Science and Marketing Strategy," in *Marketing and the Computer,* W. Alderson and S. J. Shapiro (eds.) (Englewood Cliffs, N. J.: Prentice-Hall, 1963), pp. 98–127.

[182] Wells, W. D., and J. M. Chinsky, "Effects of Competing Messages: A Laboratory Simulation," *Journal of Marketing Research,* Vol. 2 (May 1965), pp. 141–145.

[183] Zipf, G. K., "The P_1 P_2/D Hypothesis on the Intercity Movement of Persons," *American Sociological Review,* Vol. 12 (October 1964), pp. 672–687.

Index

Ackoff, R. L., 38, 112, 115, 116, 117, 137, 154, 155, 164
Adamic, Louis, 46
Adaptive models, 156
Alderson, W., 25, 118, 133, 138
Allocation problems, 113–114
American Sheep Producers Council, 83–85
Analysis, cluster, 94, 105–106
content, 58–61
correlation, 94–97
objectives of, 95
covariance, 88–91
factor, 94, 101–104
objectives of, 102–103
multiple discriminant, 94, 98–101
objectives of, 98–99
regression, 94–97
objectives of, 95
risk, 26–29
Anderson, R. L., 96
Anderson, T. W., 105
Audits and Surveys, 7

Balderston, F. E., 141–143
Bancroft, T. A., 96
Banks, A. S., 54, 73, 91, 101
Bayesian decision theory, 8–31, 116, 139
capital planning, 26
conceptual advantages of, 30–31
cost, 21–22
courses of action, 20–21
current state of, 23–31
essentials of, 9–10
extent of use of, 29
implications of, 18–22
manager-researcher dialogue, 22–23
new product introduction, 23–26

Bayesian decision theory, problem identification, 19–20
reliability of, 21–22
risk analysis, 26–29
simplified application of, 10–23
Becknell, J., Jr., 88
Behavioral measurement techniques, 32–67
buying behavior, 33–38
content analysis, 58–61
current status of, 65–66
experimental gaming, 62–65
marketing policy, 33–38
scales, 38–58
applications of techniques, 44–55
classification of methods, 41–44
Guttman's technique, 46–50
interval, 40–41
judgment methods, 42–46
limitations of, 56–58
measurement, 38–39
nominal, 39
ordinal, 39–41
Q-sort technique, 54–55
rating, 54
ratio, 40–41
reliability of, 57–58
response methods, 42, 43–44
semantic differential, 50–53
Thurstone's comparative judgment technique, 44–46
types of, 39–41
validity of, 56–57
sociogram analysis, 61–62
Benson, P. H., 46
Bernstein, A., 59, 60
Boyd, H. W., Jr., 96–97, 102
Brand-switching models, 124–127, 145, 148

179